COMBAT STRATEGIES

FOR

APEX

LEGENDS
PLAYERS

AN UNOFFICIAL GUIDE TO VICTORY

JASON R. RICH

Racehorse Publishing

Copyright © 2019 by Hollan Publishing

Apex Legends® is a registered trademark of Electronic Arts Inc.

The Apex Legends game is copyright © Electronic Arts Inc.

Racehorse Publishing books may be purchased in bulk at special discounts for sales promotion, corporate gifts, fund-raising, or educational purposes. Special editions can also be created to specifications. For details, contact the Special Sales Department, Skyhorse Publishing, 307 West 36th Street, 11th Floor, New York, NY 10018 or info@skyhorsepublishing.com.

Racehorse Publishing™ is a pending trademark of Skyhorse Publishing, Inc.®, a Delaware corporation.

Visit our website at www.skyhorsepublishing.com.

10 9 8 7 6 5 4 3 2 1

Library of Congress Cataloging-in-Publication Data is available on file.

Cover design by Brian Peterson
Cover photograph by Getty Images
Interior photographs by Jason R. Rich

ISBN: 978-1-63158-546-3
eISBN: 978-1-63158-547-0

Printed in the United States of America

TABLE OF CONTENTS

OVERVIEW OF APEX LEGENDS

Welcome to the world of *Apex Legends*! Buckle up and get ready for a heart-pounding, challenging, and visually stunning gaming experience that takes battle royale games to the next level!

SURE, THERE ARE A BUNCH OF TRULY AWESOME, MULTI-player, battle royale combat games to experience on a PC, Xbox One, or PlayStation 4 that offer intense action, non-stop challenges, and a wide range of unique gameplay experiences. Epic's *Fortnite: Battle Royale* and *PlayerUnknown's Battlegrounds* (*PUBG*) are just two extremely popular examples.

Starting in February 2019, when it was first released, EA's *Apex Legends* (developed by Respawn Entertainment) quickly captured the world's attention and attracted more than 25 million gamers in just one week. The *Apex Legends* gaming community has been expanding ever since! By mid-March 2019, the game attracted more than 50 million gamers.

Apex Legends welcomes players into the future to experience a colorful, squad-based combat adventure. It requires gamers to continuously explore potentially deadly terrain; amass and use a powerful fighting arsenal; successfully interact with squad mates; and participate in high-intensity, fast-paced battles seen from a vivid first-person perspective.

During each match, your three-person squad will compete against 19 other three-person squads. In other words, there are 60 gamers participating in real-time during each match. The sole objective is to be the last soldier alive (or the last squad alive) at the end of each match. Only then will you earn the title of "Champion." Thus, focusing on survival skills is often more important than racking up a high kill count.

DISCOVER WHAT MAKES *APEX LEGENDS* UNIQUE

Unlike other battle royale games, from a visual standpoint, all of the action in *Apex Legends* is seen from a first-person perspective. The focus is on what's happening directly in front of the futuristic soldier you're controlling.

Several things make *Apex Legends* stand out from other battle royale games. For starters, all matches are experienced as a three-player squad. You can team up with gamers you know, or have the game select squad mates for you randomly.

Plus, instead of controlling a random soldier during a match, you're forced to choose from one of the eight initial characters, called "Legends," each of whom has a unique skillset. (Starting in March 2019, EA/Respawn Entertainment began introducing additional Legends into the game.)

Prior to each match, it's important for each gamer to select a Legend that'll complement the others in their squad. Creating a well-balanced squad is a critical first challenge. As soon a match begins, it's then the responsibility of each squad member to carry their own weight, utilize their unique skills, and build their own powerful arsenal. Most importantly, squad mates need to communicate clearly, work together, protect each other, and when necessary, fight as a cohesive unit.

Each Legend's unique skillset includes a Passive, Tactical, and Ultimate ability that sets them apart from one another.

Beyond the unique fighting and defensive skills each Legend possesses, during a match, dozens of specialized weapons, weapon attachments, loot items, and soldier armor can be found, collected, and ultimately used.

In addition to controlling just your Legend (soldier) during a match. Success requires you to utilize your Legend's unique skills while working as part of a well-balanced

While finding and collecting many different types of weapons, weapon attachments, compatible ammo, loot items, and armor pieces is certainly beneficial, each Legend can only carry so much at any given time. Thus, developing inventory management skills is necessary, since you always want your Legend to be armed with an appropriate arsenal, based on the fighting situations they're about to encounter in the type of terrain they're currently in.

Your squad mates are your fighting and defensive partners. A squad that loses one or two members is at a huge disadvantage, especially when facing squads where all three members are still alive and working together as a cohesive unit. If you look in the bottom-left corner of the screen (shown here on a PC), you can see that all three squad members are alive and in good health.

Which weapon attachments are used in conjunction with guns determines the weapon's capabilities. Learning to build and maintain the most powerful arsenal possible is another essential skill that'll help your Legend and squad achieve victory.

Shown here, the soldier this gamer is controlling is using a Syringe. Meanwhile, one of the squad members has been killed, leaving just two squad mates alive.

Sharing weapons, weapon attachments, ammo, armor, and loot items with squad mates is often necessary. Equally important is taking the time to revive squad mates who get "knocked" (injured) and are rendered unable to fight (but remain alive).

When you or a squad mate gets killed in action (and this is likely to happen often), all is not lost. If a surviving squad mate locates and grabs a deceased Legend's "Banner," and successfully gets it to a Respawn Beacon within about 100 seconds, the fallen squad member will be returned to the match.

Even if you've previously mastered other battle royale games, like *PUBG* or *Fortnite: Battle Royale*, you'll quickly discover that *Apex Legends* offers some exciting new twists and gaming elements that'll keep you on your toes!

GET TO KNOW THE LEGENDS

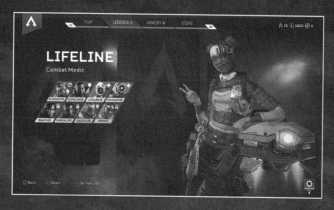

When *Apex Legends* first launched, the game featured eight unique Legend characters, including: Bloodhound, Gibraltar, Lifeline, Pathfinder, Wrath, Bangalore, Caustic, and Mirage. (You'll need to spend some money to unlock Caustic and Mirage.) A ninth Legend, called Octane, was added to the game in March 2019. You'll learn more about him in "Section 9—Take Advantage of Apex Legends Battle Passes." As the game evolves and upgrades are released, EA and Respawn Entertainment plan to introduce new Legends into the game, so stay tuned!

At the start of each match, each Legend's Health meter is pre-set to 100. Using special items and armor, it's possible to boost the Health meter up to 200. However, each time a Legend gets shot or injured some of their Health gets depleted. The Health meter for the Legend you're controlling is shown in the bottom-left corner of the main game screen. The Health and Shield meters for your squad mates are displayed in a slightly smaller format, directly above your Legend's Health and Shield meters.

A Legend's Shield meter starts off at zero (nonfunctioning). To activate and maintain your soldier's Shields for added protection against incoming attacks, you'll need find and grab body armor, and then use shield replenishment items, such as a Shield Battery, Shield Cell, or Phoenix Kit. A Legend's Shield meter is displayed directly above their Health meter. Its color determines the level of protection that's being offered, based on the level of the Body Shield being worn.

Keep in mind, a downed Legend who is not revived in time, or who is the recipient of additional attacks, will be killed. At this point, a squad member needs to help them respawn, which is a more difficult and time-consuming task that'll be explained later.

The focus of "Section 2—Meet the Legends," is on introducing you to each of the Legends and teaching you about their unique abilities, strengths, and weaknesses. It takes time and practice to get acquainted with and be able to make full use of each Legend's unique abilities.

When a Legend's Health meter hits zero, they're considered "downed" or "knocked." This means they can move around and Ping, but can't fight. While in this state, a squad member can revive the injured Legend, which is a process that takes seven seconds, during which time both the injured soldier and the soldier doing the reviving are both vulnerable to attack.

Each Legend falls into a category. When viewing the Legends screen, you'll see a thumbnail image of each Legend. In the top-right corner of the thumbnail is an icon which graphically depicts what type of soldier that Legend is. For example, Bloodhound is a Tracker, while Lifeline is a Healer and Support soldier. Gibraltar is a defensive soldier, while Wrath, Bangalore, and Mirage are more aggressive Attackers.

As a newb (beginner), get to know and practice using one Legend at a time. Don't try to master all of them at once. You'll be a much better asset to your squad if you go into each match with plenty of experience controlling a specific Legend.

Before each match begins, your squad lineup is displayed, along with details about the gamers controlling each squad member. Pay attention to who is the highest level player and follow their lead if you're a newb.

At the start of a match, it's the Jumpmaster who decides when the squad will leap from the airplane (the Jump Ship) and determines where the entire squad will land. However, any squad mate can break apart from the squad during freefall and land where they'd like. This is often counterproductive to working as a team and staying together. The assigned Jumpmaster's screenname is displayed near the bottom-center of the screen once the squad enters into the plane.

LEARN YOUR WAY AROUND KINGS CANYON

> ⚠ **MIRAGE**
> When an enemy shoots your Decoy, the enemy's position is momentarily revealed to your entire team.

At least initially, all matches take place within a vast gaming arena (an island) known as Kings Canyon. As you'll discover, it's comprised of many different regions, and each region contains different types of terrain and terrain-based challenges. As soon as you start playing *Apex Legends*, invest some time getting to know the Kings Canyon map and the different areas you'll soon be exploring and fighting in.

When each match kicks off, the entire Kings Canyon arena is safe to explore. However, shortly after each match begins, the safe area slowly begins getting smaller, which forces the remaining Legends into closer proximity.

Staying within the safe area is important to your Legend's health and well-being. Embarking into the unsafe area (or getting caught there) will be extremely detrimental to your soldier's Health meter.

Pay attention to the map screen to determine where the safe area currently is, and where the safe area will be as the match progresses. By the End Game (the final few minutes of a match), the safe area will be extremely small. During this phase of a match (if your Legend is still alive), plan on participating in close-range firefights, since all surviving Legends will be in close proximity.

At the time *Apex Legends* launched, no vehicles were available on the island. One way to quickly get around, however, is to hop a ride on a zipline. Throughout Kings Canyon, a network of ziplines already exists. However, one of Pathfinder's special abilities, as you'll soon discover, is that he can create new ziplines almost anywhere that he and other Legends (including enemies) can then use.

Be sure to check out "Section 5—What to Expect within Kings Canyon," to learn more about Kings Canyon and how to read the map and mini-map that are available during each match.

When *Apex Legends* first launched, approximately 20 different types of guns were available, including an assortment of Pistols, Shotguns, Sniper Rifles, Submachine Guns (SMGs), Assault Rifles (ARs), and Light Machine Guns (LMGs).

UNDERSTAND YOUR ARSENAL

Each type of gun has a special type of compatible ammo, and without an ample supply of that ammo, the weapon is rendered useless. Types of ammo include: Heavy Rounds, Light Rounds, Shotgun Shells, and Energy Ammo.

Shown here, a weapon is about to be picked up and added to the soldier's arsenal at the start of a match. As you can see by looking at the bottom-right corner of the screen, he's currently unarmed.

To enhance the capabilities of each type of gun, special weapon attachments (such as the 4x-8x Variable Sniper Scope that's shown here) can be added. Different types of weapon attachments can improve a gun's aim, reduce recoil, expand how much ammo it can hold, and/or reduce its reload time, for example. Weapon attachments need to be found and collected separately from weapons and ammo.

Every type of gun requires a compatible type of ammunition in order to function. Be sure to collect and stockpile ammo for the guns in your Legend's current arsenal. At any given time, a Legend can carry two guns, along with a selection of throwable weapons and other items. Only one of the two guns can be active, but it's easy to switch between weapons.

Along with guns and each Legend's special abilities, *Apex Legends* includes a selection of throwable grenades, including an Arc Star (shown here), Frag Grenade, and Thermite Grenade.

APEX LEGENDS IS A FREE GAME

To get started playing *Apex Legends*, there's nothing to buy initially, although the game does offer optional in-game purchases that you'll learn more about shortly.

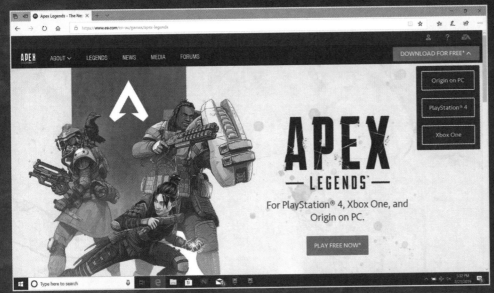

PC gamers simply need to visit the official *Apex Legends* website (www.ea.com/games/apex-legends) and click on the Download for Free button that's displayed in the top-right corner of the browser window. You'll need to set up a free, online-based Origin account (www.origin.com) to play the game once it's downloaded and installed.

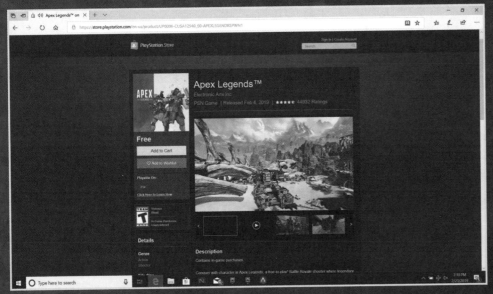

To download the game on the Xbox One, from your Internet-connected gaming system, visit the Microsoft Store. Keep in mind, a paid subscription to the Xbox Live Gold service is required to play *Apex Legends*. PlayStation 4 gamers should download the game, for free, from the PlayStation Store directly from their Internet-connected gaming console.

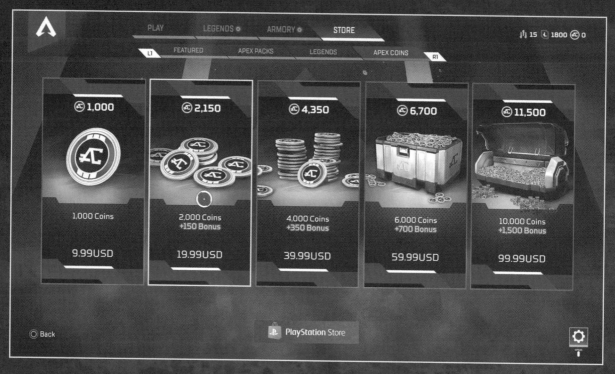

Using real money, within the *Apex Legends* Store, you're able to purchase bundles of coins. As you can see here, 1,000 coins cost $9.99 (US), 2,150 coins cost $19.95 (US), 4,350 coins cost $39.99 (US), 6,700 coins cost $59.99 (US), and 11,500 coins cost $99.00 (US).

From the Store, coins are used to purchase Featured Items, Apex Packs, and to unlock additional Legends. Apex Packs are collections of cosmetic items that include weapon skins, legend skins, banners, quips (audibles), and other items.

A GAMING HEADSET IS HIGHLY RECOMMENDED

You'll quickly discover that sound is an extremely important element in *Apex Legends*. During a match, you'll need to clearly hear the sound effects and character narration. Since this is exclusively a squad-based game, you'll also need to continuously communicate with your two squad mates. Thus, using an optional, high-quality gaming headset is extremely useful and highly recommended!

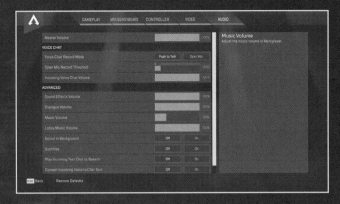

Gaming headsets have a built-in microphone. They are available from a wide range of manufacturers. Some of the more popular gaming headsets used by top-ranked *Apex Legends* gamers come from companies like Logitech G (www.logitechg.com), HyperX (www.hyperxgaming.com/us/headsets), Razer (www.razer.com/gaming-headsets-and-audio), and Turtle Beach Corp. (www.turtlebeach.com). Shown here is a partial lineup of Logitech G headsets, which range in price from $59.99 (US) to $139.99 (US). These are compatible with PCs and all popular console-based gaming systems.

Before participating in matches, one of the first things you want to do upon installing *Apex Legends* is to access the game's Settings menu and adjust the audio-related settings (shown here on a PC). Leave the Master Volume, Sound Effects Volume, and Dialogue Volume at 100 percent, but turn down the Music Volume (to 50 percent or lower, based on personal preference). Many top-ranked gamers turn off the game's music altogether to avoid its distraction. If you're using a gaming headset, also turn off the Subtitles and Convert Incoming Voice to Chat Text option.

CONSIDER UPGRADING YOUR GAMING GEAR

The reaction time of your keyboard/mouse combo or controller also impacts your success when playing *Apex Legends*. For this reason, serious gamers often opt to upgrade their equipment to include a specialty gaming keyboard and mouse for their PC, and/or a more precision-oriented controller for their console-based gaming system.

These are optional purchases that you might want to make after you've played *Apex Legends* for a while, you've tweaked the game controls (in Settings), and you believe your gaming abilities will improve with higher-end equipment.

For some gamers, a keyboard/mouse combo offers the most precise and responsive control options, especially if you're using a specialty gaming keyboard and mouse, such as those offered by Corsair (www.corsair.com), Logitech (www.logitechg.com), or Razer www.razer.com/gaming-keyboards). The Razer Huntsman Elite WR (2018) for the PC ($199.99) is shown here.

It's also possible for PC gamers to connect an Xbox One controller to their PC and then use the controller alone (or in conjunction with their keyboard/mouse) to control everything in the game. A wireless or corded Xbox One controller can be used.

Several companies, including Razer (www.razer.com/gaming-keyboards), offer one-handed, reduced-sized gaming keyboards, which feature fewer keys than a traditional keyboard, making it easier to reach only the keys needed to play a specific game, such as *Apex Legends*.

The Razer Orbweaver Chroma, for example, is priced at $129.99 (US). In addition to awesome LED colored lighting effects, it offers 30 programmable keys (which includes 20 programable mechanical keys). Priced at $34.95, the Fist Wizard One-Handed Gaming Keyboard (https://groovythingstobuy.com/products/fist-wizard-one-handed-gaming-keyboard-1) is a

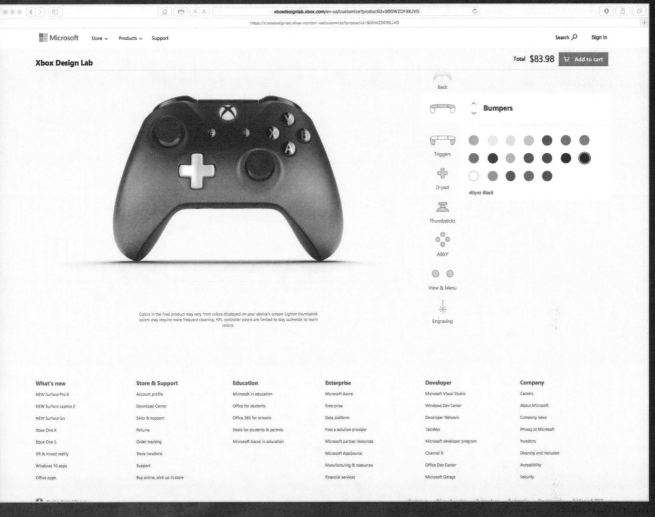

Microsoft offers a service that allows you to custom design a wireless or corded Xbox One controller. These controllers look different cosmetically but offer the same functionality as the controller that comes with the gaming system. The price varies, based on options you choose. Check out https://xboxdesignlab.xbox.com/en-us to learn more about this option.

Offering more precision than a standard console controller, several companies, such as SCUF Gaming (www.scufgaming.com), manufacture specialty Xbox One and PS4 controllers designed to cater to the needs of advanced gamers. The SCUF Impact controller for the PS4 ($139.95 US) is shown here.

Some believe these specialized controllers provide a slight advantage when playing *Apex Legends* because they offer added precision and better response time. Using one of these controllers is a matter of personal preference (based on your budget).

Xbox One or PS4 console-based gamers can use the standard wireless controllers that came bundled with their gaming system, or upgrade to more advanced controllers. It's also possible to connect a gaming keyboard and mouse directly to a console-based system. The Turret for Xbox One gaming keyboard and mouse ($249.99 US) from Razer is shown here.

Regardless of the gaming hardware you're using, memorize the controls for *Apex Legends* and keep practicing using those controls so you develop your muscle memory for the game. When you're able to rely on your muscle memory, you'll be able to react faster without having to think about which key or button to press to accomplish specific tasks.

A FAST INTERNET CONNECTION IS ESSENTIAL WHEN PLAYING *APEX LEGENDS*

If you have a slower Internet connection, you'll benefit from reducing the display resolution of the game from the Settings menu, regardless of whether you're playing *Apex Legends* on a PC (shown here) or console-based system.

From the Settings menu, highlight and select the Video submenu tab, and then adjust each option, based on the equipment you're using and the level of detail you want to see. If you know you have a slower Internet connection and/or a lower-end computer, you'll benefit from reducing the resolution and quality of the graphics generated by the game.

While the graphics won't look as awesome in a lower resolution, the speed of the game and your Legend's reaction time will improve.

CONSIDER AN ETHERNET CONNECTION TO THE INTERNET

All current model Windows PCs and console-based gaming systems have the ability to connect to the Internet via a wireless

(Wi-Fi) connection or using a physical Ethernet cable that connects between your computer (or gaming console) and modem (or a router). A wired connection is sometimes more reliable and faster than a wireless connection, and the improved speed could positively impact your game play.

For computers that don't have an Ethernet port built-in, an inexpensive Ethernet adapter can be purchased online or from popular consumer electronics stores. The Xbox One and PS4 both have Ethernet ports built into the systems, but a standard Ethernet cable (they come in many different lengths) needs to be purchased separately.

If you notice your Internet slows down, this will often cause *Apex Legends* to glitch during game play. When this happens, especially during an intense firefight or at the wrong moment, you could find your Legend dying for no good reason.

PREPARE TO JUGGLE MULTIPLE GAMING SKILLS AND TASKS SIMULTANEOUSLY

Apex Legends requires gamers to juggle a wide range of tasks simultaneously, making this much more than a straightforward first-person shooter. The top 10 challenges you'll need to contend with during every match include:

1. Choosing the best Legend based on your unique and personal gaming style and experience.
2. Creating a nicely balanced squad, so the special abilities and strengths of each Legend complement each other. With eight different Legends to choose from, there are many different possible combinations when selecting your three-person squad.
3. Working as a cohesive team. This means staying in constant communication with your squad mates, working together both offensively and defensively, and using the game's Ping feature (which will be explained later) when appropriate. The focus of "Section 7—Strategies for Working and Communicating with Your Squad," is on how to effectively work with your squad mates during a match.
4. Safely exploring Kings Canyon while taking advantage of the terrain you're in and avoiding the unique challenges and obstacles offered in each area.
5. Finding, acquiring, managing, and using your soldier's arsenal of weapons, weapon attachments, and ammo. This not only requires you to locate and grab weapons and related components (while stockpiling compatible ammo), it also means knowing which weapon to use based on your current situation. "Section 6—Building and Using Your Arsenal," explains the different types of weapons and weapon attachments available and how to best use them.
6. Collecting and properly using loot items and Health/Shield

replenishment items.

7. Protecting your Legend using the best collection of armor.

8. Keeping you Legend and your squad mates healthy and alive during a match.

9. Knowing how and when to use your Legend's special abilities.

10. Managing your Legend's inventory. This requires you to acquire everything you'll need, based on the situations you anticipate encountering, and dropping weapons, weapon attachments, loot items, and ammo, for example, that you no longer need, don't want, or that are just taking up valuable inventory space.

11. Being successful during each match has a cumulative impact on your Player Level, which increases by accruing XP (Experience Points). By leveling up, you'll be able to unlock and earn various types of rewards, such as Apex Packs and Legend Tokens. Real money can also be spent on cosmetic upgrades to your soldier, but these have zero impact on their in-game capabilities.

XP is earned by achieving kills, injuring (knocking) enemies, remaining alive as long as possible during matches, Reviving or Respawning squad mates, and for achieving specific other tasks.

STAY TUNED: *APEX LEGENDS* CONTINUES TO EVOLVE

As with any game in the battle royale genre, the game's publisher periodically releases updates that can introduce new locations within Kings Canyon; entirely new arenas; additional weapons, weapon attachments, loot items, armor, and health items; new Legends; and exciting new game play elements and challenges.

To stay up-to-date on the latest additions to *Apex Legends*, be sure to visit the game's official News webpage (www.ea.com/games/apex-legends/news). Also, consider following the official *Apex Legends* Twitter and Instagram accounts (@PlayApex), plus check out the other online-based resources listed within "Section 10—*Apex Legends* Resources."

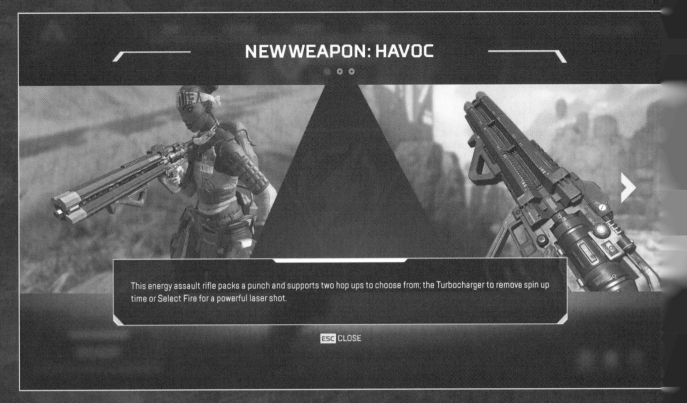

NEW WEAPON: HAVOC

This energy assault rifle packs a punch and supports two hop ups to choose from; the Turbocharger to remove spin up time or Select Fire for a powerful laser shot.

ESC CLOSE

From the Lobby screen within the game, click or select the News icon to quickly discover what's new within *Apex Legends*. Of course, you always want to ensure you have the latest version of the game installed onto your PC, PS4, or Xbox One. Each time you load the game, it will automatically check to see if an update is available and required.

This unofficial strategy guide will help you develop a better understanding of the game plus teach you hundreds of proven strategies that'll help you stay alive longer, kill more enemies, and ultimately win more matches.

SECTION 2
MEET THE LEGENDS

SELECT LEGEND

3

YOU ARE PICKING

1ST

jasonrich7

As a gamer, your first major decision at the start of each *Apex Legends* match is to choose your Legend.

BLOODHOUND

YOUR SQUAD

Because each has their own specialty, along with three unique abilities, the Legend you choose will determine your role in your squad.

After each gamer has locked in their decision for which Legend they'll control, the Your Squad screen is displayed.

EACH LEGEND HAS A TACTICAL ABILITY THAT ONCE USED, REQUIRES TIME TO RECHARGE OR COOLDOWN BEFORE IT CAN BE used again. The Legend's unique **passive ability** always remains active and can be used as often as you'd like during each match. The Legend's **ultimate ability** takes extra time to charge. You can, however, find and use a consumable Ultimate Accelerant item. It allows your

Caustic's tactical ability, for example, is called Nox Gas Trap. It allows him to set traps containing poisonous gas that enemies automatically activate when in close proximity. However, by shooting at the trap, Caustic (or any Legend) can detonate the trap from a distance. If you're detonating the trap to inflict damage on enemies from a distance, this is useful. If you're trying to protect yourself from receiving damage from a trap set by an enemy, shoot the trap from a distance before you get too close and detonate it.

You can't rely on just your Legend's unique abilities to win firefights or matches. Ultimately, you'll need to utilize armor for protection, Health-related items to stay alive, and most importantly, build and use a well-rounded and powerful weapon arsenal. Shown here is a purple Body Shield that's about to be picked up and worn by the soldier for protection. This is an important type of armor.

Mixing and matching your Legend's unique abilities with the use of regular weapons during a firefight will give you the best advantage. Many gamers, however, forget to use their Legend's unique abilities in conjunction with regular weapons because they get caught up in the excitement of a firefight.

While it's an excellent strategy to keep controlling one Legend so that you become an expert working with that character, it's equally important to understand what sets each Legend apart, so you're able to put together and then successfully fight within a well-balanced squad.

KEEP YOUR LEGEND MOVING

During each match, a Legend has the ability move freely in any direction using the directional controls on your keyboard/mouse or a controller. In addition to walking, a Legend can run, crouch, interact with objects, pick up items, aim a weapon, fire a weapon, reload a weapon, toss a grenade, holster their weapon, Ping, use their unique abilities, jump, punch, kick, or climb, for example.

In general, and especially when your Legend is out in the open, avoid standing still for more than a few seconds at a time. When walking or running, avoid traveling in a straight line. Follow a random, zig-zag pattern and use the Slide-Jump maneuver periodically to make your soldier a tougher moving target to hit. Simply jumping up and down like you would in other battle royale games will make your Legend stand out and attract unwanted attention.

Whenever possible, use your surroundings to provide cover. You can crouch behind walls or objects to make your Legend smaller, more difficult to spot, and harder to target with weapons. On the left, the soldier is standing behind a wall of sandbags ready to shoot enemies in front of him. On the right, he's crouching behind those same sandbags for protection.

Maintaining a height advantage during a firefight almost always puts you at an advantage, makes it easier to target enemies, and makes it harder for enemies to return fire accurately. You'll discover all sorts of things your Legend can climb up on in order to achieve a height advantage.

TAKE ADVANTAGE OF ARMOR

A Body Shield is one type of armor your Legend can utilize. This type of gear is available in four levels, which determines how much additional shielding (protection) it'll offer.

A level 1 (Common) Body Shield adds two bars (50HP) to your Legend's Shield and has a white hue. A level 2 (Rare) Body Shield adds three bars (75HP) to your Legend's Shield and is displayed with a blue hue (shown

Body Shield also adds four bars (100HP) to your Legend's Shield. A level 4 Body Shield, however, also recharges completely each time you kill an enemy. It has a gold hue.

A second essential piece of armor you want to find and provide to your Legend is a Helmet. These too come in four color-coded levels. A level 1 Helmet, with its white hue, is shown here. The purpose of a Helmet is to protect your soldier from headshots. Typically, a direct headshot causes the most injury (damage) to a soldier's Health meter. A Helmet reduces the damage incurred.

A level 1 (white) helmet reduces headshot damage by 30 percent. A level 2 (blue) Helmet reduces headshot damage by 40 percent. A level 3 (purple) Helmet reduces headshot damage by 50 percent. Meanwhile, a level 4 (gold) Helmet not only reduces headshot damage by 50 percent, is also reduces the charge/recharge time for your Legend's unique tactical and ultimate abilities.

The third type of armor, called a Knockdown Shield, is used to keep your Legend alive longer once their Health meter hits zero and they're considered "knocked down." While a soldier is in the knocked down state, by pressing the Fire button, you can activate their Knockdown Shield to provide extra shielding in front of them. This provides added protection from continued attacks until the injured soldier can be revived. It can also give them more time for squad mates to arrive and render assistance.

A level 1 (white) Knockdown Shield has 100HP. A level 2 (blue) Knockdown Shield has 250 HP. A level 3 (purple) Knockdown Shield has 750HP, while a level 4 (gold) Knockdown Shield also has 750 HP, and it offers the ability for the knocked down Legend to revive themselves during a 10-second period. For this self-revive feature to work, the knocked down soldier can't be attacked or further injured during the Revive process.

    As quickly as you can at the start of a match, boost your Legend's defensive capabilities by finding and grabbing the strongest Helmet, Body Shield, and Knockdown Shield possible.

GRAB A BACKPACK

In addition to armor and weapons, a Backpack is an essential tool you'll want to grab and use as quickly as possible at the start of a match. There are four Backpack levels, and each determines how much additional inventory your Legend can carry at once.

Like Armor and most weapons and ammo, Backpacks are color coded for easy identification. A level 1 (Common) Backpack, displayed with a white hue, adds two extra inventory slots. A level 2 (Rare) Backpack, displayed with a blue hue, adds four slots to your Legend's inventory capacity. A level 3 (Epic) Backpack, displayed with a purple hue, adds six slots to your Legend's inventory capacity.

Ideally, you want to equip your soldier with a level 4 (Legendary) Backpack, which offers six inventory slots. It has a golden hue. This item also cuts in half the amount of time it takes to utilize Health-related consumables. This feature alone is useful, because anytime your soldier uses a Health consumable it requires several seconds, during which time they're vulnerable to attack and can't use a weapon. You can see all of the Inventory slots and what's within them by looking at your Legend's Inventory screen

TAKE ADVANTAGE OF PINGS TO COMMUNICATE

Every Legend has the ability to use the game's Ping feature. These are callouts that allow squad mates to easily communicate, without using their voice. Pings are particularly useful to gamers not using a gaming headset (with a built-in mic), but they can be used by all gamers to make communication between squad mates more efficient.

When a Ping is used, all of your squad mates will hear an audible announcement in their Legend's voice (not the gamer's voice). In some cases, a Ping will also appear as a text-based message within the in-game chat, or as a marker on the map and/or mini-map.

As you'll discover, there are a dozen types of Pings that can be used at any time during a match. Learn the keyboard key binding or controller button binding associated with Pings to make them faster and more efficient to use.

Some of the more commonly used Pings include:

- **Attacking Here**—Alert your squad mates that you're attacking one or more enemies at a specific location and ask for assistance.
- **Banner**—Once your Legend has been killed, use this Ping to tell your squad mates that you've been eliminated from the match and share the location of your Banner. If the Banner is found in time, and brought to a Respawn location, your Legend could be brought back to life and returned into the match.
- **Defending Here**—Inform your squad mates that you're currently defending a specific location and ask for their help.
- **Enemy Here**—Alert your squad mates that you've spotted an enemy and show the enemy's location.
- **Going Here**—Tell your squad mates where you're headed and mark that location on the map.
- **Help**—This Ping is only available once your Legend is knocked down. Use it to broadcast a message asking for immediate assistance.
- **Looting Here**—When you discover a location with useful loot items to collect, use this Ping to inform your squad mates that you're looting at a specific location.
- **Someone's Been Here**—Warn your squad mates that an area you're in is not safe because an enemy has clearly been there (and may still be there waiting to launch an ambush).

It's also possible to Ping specific locations, ammo, enemies, weapons, equipment, weapon attachments, as well as some objects.

GET TO KNOW THE EIGHT ORIGINAL LEGENDS

When *Apex Legends* first launched, the game included eight original Legends. The following is useful information about those original eight Legends. Check out "Section 9—Take Advantage of Apex Legends Battle Passes" for details about Octane, who was added a few weeks after Apex Legends first launched. He's one of the Legends you need to pay for in order to unlock.

Once you choose to become an expert controlling a specific Legend, keep practicing with that character until you're really good at using their special abilities in a wide range of situations and you're able to nicely combine the use of traditional weapons with the Legend's unique abilities.

After you've unlocked all of the available Legends from the Store, this message will appear. Don't get too complacent, however. It'll just be a matter of time before new Legends are introduced into the game—each offering new special abilities and fighting skills.

BANGALORE

Bangalore is an attacker. She's the perfect Legend to choose if you enjoy fighting, while staying very mobile. While she can be the lead soldier in a battle, she can also offer strong support to her squad mates, should the need arise. Be sure to equip Bangalore with an Assault Rifle and/or SMG to enhance her fighting abilities from mid-range. In close range, she has the ability to work nicely with Frag Grenades and Shotguns, for example.

Her tactical ability is Smoke Launcher. This smoke can be used to cloud an area, making it harder for enemies to see and find their way, or successfully see and accurately target Bangalore's squad mates. Smoke can also be used to hide squad mates or divert enemy attention when a quick escape is required. Smoke Launcher can be shot into a confined space occupied by enemies to cause confusion and wreak havoc.

As you can see from the bottom of the screen, her passive ability is Double Time. This allows her to move extra quickly between locations. It's useful when she needs to pass through open areas, because Double Time makes it harder for enemies to successfully target and hit her. This Double Time ability is also useful when the squad needs her to sneak off and then flank enemies while her squad mates approach from another direction.

Her ultimate ability is Rolling Thunder. This ability allows her to drop a powerful airstrike over enemy territory and potentially injure multiple enemies at once. At the same time that Bangalore uses this ability, her squad mates can provide additional weapons fire toward the target area, but from a distance. Keep in mind, there is a slight delay between when this weapon is deployed and when it detonates, so plan accordingly. Also, since Rolling Thunder is launched with a toss, keep in mind it can't be sent too far off into the distance.

BLOODHOUND

Bloodhound is a tracker. He's a great addition to any squad, because he'll help locate enemies. This knowledge can be used to plan and execute attacks, or to avoid enemies when you and your squad are outgunned or vulnerable. All of Bloodhound's special abilities are based on tracking enemies, so use them wisely, especially when planning ambushes.

His tactical ability is Eye of the Allfather. Use this to pinpoint the location of enemies within close range, even if they're hiding behind walls or within buildings.

His passive ability is Tracker. When used, footsteps appear in the area, indicating where enemies have recently been and in what direction they were traveling. This ability requires you to pay attention to the clues, so you're able to follow the path of enemies in motion. Keep your eyes peeled to the ground so you can see the footsteps that Tracker reveals. Unfortunately, if the enemy that's being tracked is able to take to the air (using a zipline, for example), their tracks will come to an abrupt halt.

His ultimate ability is Beast of the Hunt. For a limited period, this ability reveals the location of enemies in the area and allows Bloodhound to temporarily move faster. Ultimately, Bloodhound's special abilities work best when he's teamed up with Legends who have strong attack capabilities.

CAUSTIC

Caustic is a defensive Legend whose specialty is close-range combat. This makes him particularly useful during the End Game (the final minutes of a match) when the safe area is small and all remaining soldiers are in close proximity.

Caustic is one of the Legends you must pay real money to unlock. This can be done using 12,000 Legend Tokens or 750 Apex Coins (approximately $9.99 US). This Legend's ability to set traps makes him useful for maintaining control over a specific area or region. Traps can surprise and injure enemies as they're coming through doorways or hiding in enclosed spaces.

His tactical ability is Nox Gas Trap. Set a trap that'll injure enemies who get caught in the toxic gas cloud upon its detonation. The trap will activate when an enemy approaches, or it activates immediately upon being shot at. Unfortunately, if it's shot by an enemy from a distance, the trap can be destroyed before it causes any damage. These traps work best when they're placed in hidden locations or in spots where that can't be spotted until the enemy is too close to do anything about it.

Consider using a Nox Gas Trap to block a doorway and potentially trap an enemy within a room or structure. His passive ability is Nox Vision. While his enemies are stuck in a cloud of toxic smoke, Caustic can see through the gas and not be injured by it, so he can quickly approach enemies and launch a potentially deadly assault while their vision and mobility are impaired.

His tactical ability is Dome of Protection. This ability allows Gibraltar to create an impenetrable energy dome to protect himself and his squad mates. Use it to prevent damage from an incoming attack. The drawback is that those being protected on the inside of the dome can't use their weapons to fire out toward enemies.

His ultimate ability is Nox Gas Grenade. When this unique grenade is tossed, the area where it lands will quickly be filled by a cloud of toxic smoke. It'll visually impair enemies while causing harm to their health. This weapon is best used when it's tossed into a confined space where enemies are inside. It can also be used to block a pathway or route that an enemy was planning to follow, forcing them to make a detour.

GIBRALTAR

His passive ability is Gun Shield. This is a pop-up shield that appears in front of whatever gun Gibraltar is holding. It only offers protection in front of Gibraltar. Unlike the Dome of Protection, this shield can't withstand unlimited attacks. Eventually it deactivates if it takes too much damage. When using this shield, watch your back and sides, since they remain vulnerable and unshielded.

Gibraltar is a defensive Legend. Once this guy chooses an area to defend, he's often able to hold that spot and ward off enemies—with your help, of course.

His ultimate ability is Defensive Bombardment. This weapon is somewhat like Bangalore's Rolling Thunder. It launches up into the sky, deploys, and then bombs the area below. You can theoretically deploy it above you when being attacked, and then use the Dome of Protection to protect yourself and your squad while your enemies take damage.

LIFELINE

Lifeline is a healer. Having a healer as part of a squad is always a good idea. When a squad mate needs health-related help, Lifeline can come to the rescue! She can also

serve as a support soldier in firefights when additional firepower is needed, assuming she's well-armed with weapons and ammo. When traveling in a group with a squad, Lifeline should stay in the middle or back.

Her tactical ability is D.O.C. Heal Drone. This can be used anytime during a match to heal squad mates and boost their Health, even if they're not yet knocked out. Once used, it takes about a minute to recharge, so use it wisely, when it's needed to keep your squad healthy and fit for combat.

Her passive ability is Combat Medic. When used properly, Lifeline can position herself just right and heal a squad mate while generating a protective shield around herself and the Legend she's healing. This healing method works about 25 percent faster than a typical Revive.

Her ultimate ability is Care Package. When initiated, this ability calls for a Drop Crate to be delivered that will contain a useful item. First choose where the Care Package will land. Next, wait for it to arrive.

Any nearby Legend can open the Care Package to grab what's inside.

MIRAGE

Mirage is an attacker and an expert when it comes to deception. He is one of the Legends you must pay real money to unlock.

Acquiring Mirage is done using 12,000 Legend Tokens or 750 Apex Coins (approximately $9.99 US) from the Store. Mirage is the ideal Legend to choose if you like confusing your enemies, sneaking around, and being a bit mischievous, as opposed to confronting enemies with

His tactical ability is Psyche Out. Use this ability to create a hologram of Mirage running in a straightforward direction, starting from a location you select. Simply look in the direction where you want to create the hologram and activate it. Use it to distract an enemy, lure an enemy into a location, or as a lead Legend when your squad is pushing another. The more creative you are when using this ability, the more useful it'll be.

His ultimate ability is Vanishing Act. When activated, Mirage deploys a group of holographic clones that run in different directions, while at the same time, the real Mirage is able to cloak himself and travel in another direction altogether. The nearby enemies will waste time and ammo shooting at the holograms, while the real Mirage is hopefully able to escape undetected. The drawback is that if you see a bunch of Mirage holograms, as the opponent, you should know to just ignore them and wait for the real version of Mirage to reappear.

PATHFINDER

Even during freefall, Mirage has the ability to send out clones to confuses the enemy about where his squad plans to land. Simply select the Use Decoy command during freefall to launch the clones. His passive ability is Encore! Anytime Mirage gets knocked down and then an enemy approaches to attack, this ability allows him to create a holographic decoy and then cloak himself for five seconds. When the hologram of Mirage runs off, the hope is that the enemy will follow, leaving the real Mirage safely behind where he can wait for a squad mate to revive him.

Pathfinder is a healer and a robot. He's not at all menacing from an appearance standpoint, but he should not be written off as a weakling. While he can perform decently in a firefight when he is properly armed, this is not the Legend you want leading a squad into combat.

His tactical ability is Grappling Hook. This is a great tool for quickly escaping out of areas in a Spider-Man–like way. He simply needs to launch his Grappling Hook onto a higher up wall or ledge, for example, and then he'll be catapulted to that location quickly. This can also be used to grab onto an enemy and pull him toward Pathfinder (causing damage in the process).

His ultimate ability is Zipline Gun. After creating a zipline almost anywhere, all Legends can then ride it to quickly reach another area. This is a great tool for providing an escape route from an area, or to quickly relocate the squad to another region. When soldiers are riding a zipline to get from one place to another, they become rather difficult targets for enemies to lock onto and hit. First select and aim the Grappling Hook where you want the zipline to end. The starting location is where Pathfinder is currently standing.

Once it's created, any Legend can ride the newly created zipline. To grab onto and ride a zipline, stand below it, look up at it, and select the Ride command.

His passive ability is Insider Knowledge. In this case, the ability can be used to preview where the next safe circle on the map will be, providing this information to his squad before others have it. This is a particularly useful skill to use toward the end of a match, when you need to get into position and be within the safe area as the final battles ensue. To use it, Pathfinder must first locate and hack into a Survey Beacon (shown here). These are labeled on the map, but only when you're controlling Pathfinder.

WRAITH

Wraith is an attacker. Thanks to her unique abilities, she's the Legend to choose if you want to sneak around and be able to launch ambushes and surprise attacks on enemies. What sets her apart is her ability to create a teleport that any Legend can then use to get from one pre-set location to another almost instantly. Choose to control Wraith if you want a soldier who can move fast and stay stealthy.

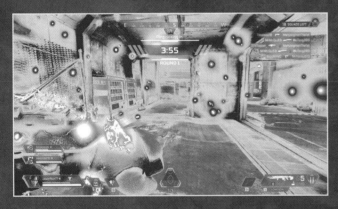

Her tactical ability is Into the Void. It allows her to move very quickly and become almost (but not completely) invisible while on the go.

Wraith's passive ability is Voices of the Void. When there's an incoming attack, this ability allows her to sense it and dodge it, often without any injury being inflicted. It's almost like having a psychic ability where a mysterious voice warns Wraith of impending danger.

Her ultimate ability is Dimensional Rift. Using this ability, Wraith can create two portals—an entrance and an exit—that any Legends can instantly pass through in order to instantly transport from one place to another.

Wraith's portals last about 60 seconds, during which time they can be used as often as they're needed. Ideally, you want to place one rift in a safe location before a battle, and then place the second in the middle of the firefight if Wraith or her squad mates need to make a quick escape. The drawback is that enemies can also use Wraith's portals. Thus, you may benefit from guarding the exit and being ready to attack those who come through. Either that or consider placing a trap near the portal's exit.

HOW TO CUSTOMIZE YOUR LEGEND

APEX LEGENDS OFFERS SEVERAL WAYS TO CUSTOMIZE A Legend's appearance and weapons, as well as their personality and the vocal phrases (Quips) they can use during a match. It's important to understand that many of these customization options cost real money, and all of them are for cosmetic purposes. None impact the actual capabilities, strength, agility, or speed of a Legend during a match.

Health-replenishment items, like this Med Kit, are important for keeping your Legend alive during a match. A Med Kit returns your Legend's Health meter to 100 percent in eight seconds.

Any items you acquire from the Store or unlock within the game are yours to keep and can be used over and over again.

ADJUSTING THE CONTROLS

From the game's Settings menu, it's possible to adjust the sensitivity of the controls, as well as other options that'll impact response times, and the appearance of game graphics, for example. After manually adjusting any of these settings, they'll remain saved until you change them again.

In order to enhance a soldier's offensive or defensive capabilities, you need to equip them with armor, weapons, weapon attachments, ammo, and Health items during each match. Shown here is a Helmet that's about to be picked up and worn by the soldier who grabs it. If the just-found Armor item is stronger than the one the Legend was already wearing, it'll automatically replace the weaker version of that item.

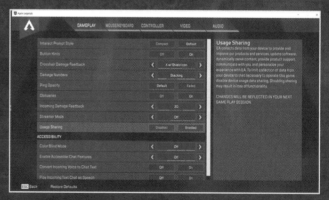

When making any changes to the Settings menu options that relate to the sensitivity of controls or the quality of the graphics, make small and subtle changes, play the game, see the impact those changes have, and then if necessary, make additional tweaks.

The Settings menu is divided into four (or five) categories—Gameplay, Mouse/Keyboard (for PC gamers and those using a keyboard/mouse with their console-based system), Controller, Video, and Audio. These are displayed along the top of the screen. From the Gameplay submenu, you can determine what information gets displayed on the screen during matches and turn off content that you feel just adds clutter to the screen.

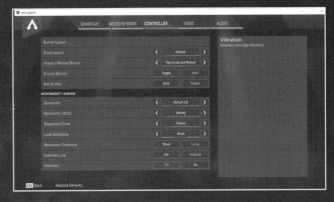

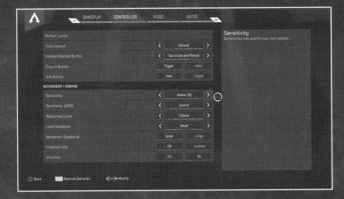

If you're using a console-based gaming system (the PS4 menu is shown here), the Controller submenu offers options that allow you to customize controller button bindings, plus adjust the Sensitivity of the controls. There's also a Sensitivity (ADS) option. For a controller, the default sensitivity of these two settings is 3. The range is between 1 (very low) and 8 (insane). Most gamers keep these two settings at the same level, so if you change one, change the other.

Also from the Controller menu, consider turning off the Vibration feature. If the controller vibrates during a firefight (which it's designed to do), the extra movement could impact your aiming precision. The Controller menu is available when playing either a console or the PC version of the game, since an optional Xbox One controller can be connected to your PC. Shown here is the PC version of the menu.

CONTROLLER BUTTON BINDINGS

The controller button bindings determine which controller button controls each feature or function available during gameplay on a PS4 or Xbox One. Whether or not you adjust these bindings is a matter of personal preference (although when the game launched, not all of them were adjustable). PC gamers, however, often opt to customize the key bindings for their keyboard and mouse.

Be sure you memorize these controls as quickly as possible and get plenty of practice using them!

DEFAULT BUTTON BINDINGS FOR THE PS4 AND XBOX ONE

COMMAND/FUNCTION	PLAYSTATION 4	XBOX ONE
Aim Down Weapon Sight	L2	Left Trigger
Charge Firing Mode (Not applicable for all weapons.)	Left Directional Button	Left Directional Button
Crouch	Circle Button	B Button
Equip Grenade	Right Directional Button	Right Directional Button
Extra Character Action	Down Directional Button	Down Directional Button
Fight	Right Stick (R3)	Right Bumper
Fire / Attack	R2	Right Trigger
Inventory	Option Button	Menu Button
Jump	X Button	A Button
Map	Touch Pad	View Button
Melee	Hold Right Stick (R3)	Hold Right Stick
Movement	Left Stick	Left Stick
Pickup / Reload / Interact / Open	Square Button	X Button
Ping	R1	Right Bumper
Ping Wheel	Hold R1	Hold Right Bumper
Run (Sprint)	Hold Left Stick (L3)	Hold Down Left Stick
Tactical Ability	L1	Left Bumper
Ultimate Ability	L1 + R1	Left Bumper + Right Bumper
Use Health Kit / Shield Kit	Up Directional Button	Up Directional Button
Weapon Change	Triangle Button	Y Button

DEFAULT KEY BINDINGS FOR A PC'S KEYBOARD AND MOUSE

COMMAND/FUNCTION	KEYBOARD KEY OR MOUSE BUTTON
Move Forward	W
Move Back	S
Move Left	A
Move Right	D
Sprint / Run	Left Shift
Jump	Space Bar
Crouch (Toggle)	C
Crouch (Hold)	Left Ctrl
Tactical Ability	Q
Ultimate Ability	Z
Alternate Interact	X
Interact / Pickup / Open	E
Inventory (Toggle)	Tab / I
Map (Toggle)	M
Attack	Left Mouse Button
Toggle Fire Mode	B
Aim Down Sight (Toggle)	Right Mouse Button
Melee	V
Reload Weapon	R
Cycle Weapon	Mouse Wheel Scroll
Equip Weapon 1	1
Equip Weapon 2	2
Holster Weapons	3
Equip Grenade	G
Use Health Item That's Selected	4
Inspect Weapon	N
Ping	Mouse Wheel Click
Push to Talk	T
Message Team	Enter

If you're playing the PC version of *Apex Legends*, the Mouse/Keyboard submenu within Settings offers options for customizing each of the key bindings and adjusting the sensitivity of the mouse. From this menu, you can add key bindings (not currently assigned) for additional Ping options.

The Video option when playing on a console-based system allows you to adjust the screen brightness and the Field of View. You may need to adjust the Screen Brightness if you switch from playing the game in a brightly lit room to a dark room, for example.

The Field of View determines how much detail you'll see off in the distance during a match. This impacts the quality of the graphics and the amount of computing power required to generate those graphics. Setting the Field of View option to the maximum level when playing the PS4 or Xbox One version

If you're playing the PC version of *Apex Legends*, the performance of the game will have a lot to do with the equipment you're using. First, make sure your PC has at least the minimum system requirements for playing the game. Assuming this is the case, if you have a lower-end PC, you may want to reduce the Resolution and Field of View, along with some of the options displayed below the Advanced heading in order to maximize computer system performance when playing and avoid unwanted glitching.

According to EA, the PC **minimum system requirements** for *Apex Legends* are:

OPERATING SYSTEM	64-BIT WINDOWS 10
CPU	Intel Core i3-6300 3.8GHz / AMD FX-4350 4.2 GHz Quad-Core Processor
RAM	6GB
GPU	NVIDIA GeForce GT 640 / Radeon HD 7700
GPU RAM	1GB
Hard Drive Space	Minimum 30 GB of free space

According to EA, the PC **recommended system requirements** for *Apex Legends* are:

OPERATING SYSTEM	64-BIT WINDOWS 10
CPU	Intel i5 3570K or equivalent
RAM	8GB
GPU	Nvidia GeForce GTX 970 / AMD Radeon R9 290
GPU RAM	8GB
Hard Drive Space	Minimum 30 GB of free space

To save time, after making any changes within Settings, from the Lobby screen (shown here), return to Training Mode to test out the impact those changes have on gameplay.

SHOPPING AT THE STORE

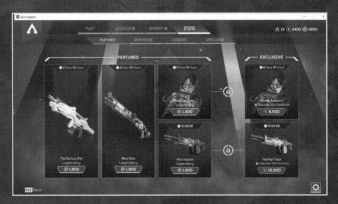

From *Apex Legend*'s Lobby screen, select the Store option to visit the online-based store. The selection of items sold here changes daily. Some cosmetic items can be acquired using Crafting Metals. Meanwhile, Legend Tokens are earned by playing *Apex Legends* and leveling up as a gamer. These can be used to unlock Legends and acquire exclusive items from the Store. It requires 600 Legend Tokens to increase a level.

One way to gather Crafting Metals is by opening Apex Packs. A Common cosmetic item typically costs 30 Crafting Metals. A Rare item costs 60 Crafting Metals. An Epic item

it makes sense to save up Crafting Metals so you can acquire Legendary items that are exclusive and not available elsewhere.

Most purchases from the Featured section of the Store require you to spend real money. First, you need to purchase Apex Coins. You can purchase bundles of between 1,000 and 11,500 coins at a time, based on how much money you want to spend. Once you've acquired Apex Coins, return to the Featured, Apex Packs, or Legends section of the Store to make purchases.

Every day, the Featured section of the Store reveals a different selection of cosmetic items you can purchase using Apex Coins (or in some cases Legend Tokens). One at a time, select the item you want to purchase, and then select the Unlock button to acquire it by spending Apex Points or Legend Tokens (whichever is applicable). From the Featured section of the Store, this Void Specialist skin for Wraith is selected. It's being sold for 1,800 Apex Coins. To purchase it (assuming you have enough coins), click on the red Unlock with 1,800 Apex Coins button.

Next, confirm your purchase by clicking on the Unlock with 1,800 Apex Coins. The item will now be added to your player account's inventory.

The Featured section of the Store typically offers Weapon Skins, Legend Skins, Banner Frames, and other cosmetic items. Some items are extremely rare (very limited edition), while others will re-appear periodically within the Store. Shown here, the Nitro Kustom weapon skin for the Devotion weapon (which is ranked as Legendary) was selected from the Featured menu and is about to be purchased for 1,800 Apex Coins.

To access the Legend's customization screen (shown here), return to the Lobby, select the Legends tab (in this case choose Wraith), and then select the Skins tab at the top of the screen. As you can see, the Void Specialist skin has now been unlocked and can be selected and worn when you opt to control Wraith during a match.

HOW TO PURCHASE AND USE APEX PACKS

Apex Packs include a random selection of three cosmetic items. Each time you purchase and open an Apex Pack, the probability of acquiring at least one Rare or better item is 100 percent. The probability of acquiring at least one Epic or Better item is 24.8 percent, and the probability of acquiring at least one Legendary item is 7.4 percent. You will never receive duplicate cosmetic items. In addition, for every 30 Apex Packs that are purchased, you're guaranteed to obtain at least one Legendary item, which are the rarest.

Apex Packs can be earned and unlocked as a result of game play or purchased for 100 Apex Coins each (approximately $1.00 US). Ten Apex Packs can be purchased at the same time for 1,000 Apex Coins (approximately $10.00 US).

Whether you earn Apex Packs from playing *Apex Legends* or purchase them from the Store, to unlock them and reveal their contents, first return to the Lobby and click on the red Apex Packs Remaining button that's displayed in the top-right corner of the screen.

Shown above are the contents of two different Apex Packs. The one shown in the top image contains a rare skin for Bloodhound, as well as two audible Quips for other Legends. In the bottom image, the Apex Pack reveals three different weapon skins.

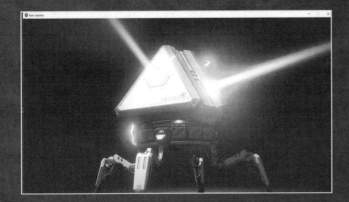

Each Apex Pack needs to be opened separately.

Once the contents of an Apex Pack is revealed, click on each item one at a time and then select the Equip button to add it to your player account, so it becomes immediately available to you.

OTHER ITEMS YOU CAN PURCHASE FROM THE STORE

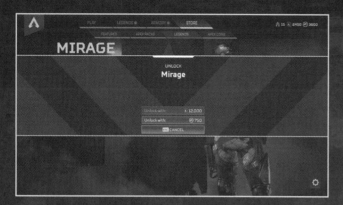

Using 12,000 Legend Tokens or 750 Apex Coins, it's possible to unlock additional Legends and make them accessible for you to select during a match. When *Apex Legends* first launched, six of the eight original Legends were unlocked and accessible to everyone. However, Caustic and Mirage needed to be unlocked from the Store. Over time, additional Legends will be introduced into the game that will need to be unlocked before they're accessible.

Starting in March 2019, *Apex Legends* Season One kicked off. In conjunction, the very first **Battle Pass** was made available as an optional (but recommended) purchase. It included the ability to unlock a new Legend, weapons, loot items, and other cosmetic items simply by playing Apex Legends. Be sure to check the News section of the official **Apex Legends** website (www.ea.com/games/apex-legends/news) for details on Battle Passes, what's included with them, and how much they cost. Also, check out Section 9 of this guide.

TAKE ADVANTAGE OF TWITCH PRIME PACKS

EA has teamed up with Twitch.tv and Amazon Prime to occasionally offer free Twitch Prime Packs. These are collections of cosmetic loot items and five Apex Packs that can be acquired and unlocked if you are a paid Amazon Prime subscriber and have a free Twitch.tv account that's linked with your *Apex Legends* gaming account. To learn more about Twitch Prime Packs, visit www.twitch.amazon.com/apex.

If you play *Apex Legends* on multiple gaming platforms, the items you receive from Twitch Prime Packs can only be associated with your account on the one gaming platform you select.

HOW TO USE ITEMS THAT HAVE BEEN PURCHASED OR UNLOCKED

Once you've unlocked or purchased items, they can be applied to various Legends prior to a match. To do this from the Lobby screen, select the Legend tab, and then choose which Legend you want to apply cosmetic items to.

Each type of cosmetic item falls into one of four categories—Skins, Banners, Quips, and Finishers. Each category tab is displayed along the top of the screen. There are also Skins available for weapons that change their appearance within the game, but not their functionality.

By unlocking one or more Skins for a specific Legend, you can alter their appearance within the game. Each Skin needs to be unlocked or purchased separately. The ones available to you will have a checkmark next to their title. All others will display a lock symbol.

To unlock a locked Skin, select it. Choose the Unlock command. You'll then be given the opportunity to unlock it with Craft Metals, Legend Tokens, or Apex Coins. If you have the right amount of in-game currency and want to make the purchase, use the Unlock button. Otherwise use the Cancel command to return to the previous screen.

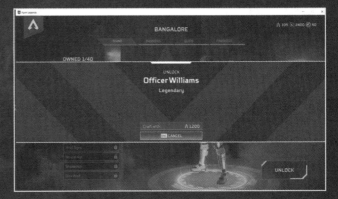

Unless Legend Skins are featured items within the Store, they typically need to be acquired using Craft Metals, not Apex Coins.

Upon selecting the Banners option, there are many additional cosmetic items that can be applied to the selected Legend. These include Frames, Poses, Badges, and Trackers. Each of these must be purchased or unlocked separately. Trackers, for example, display specific tidbits of information relating to your experience and achievements as a gamer while controlling that Legend.

Quips are the audible sayings (heard using the Legend's voice) that each Legend can use during a match. There are two types of Quips—Intros and Kill messages. Each must be purchased or unlocked separately, and then can be used during matches to communicate with or taunt enemies. Shown here are the Quips menus for Pathfinder and Wraith. As you can see, most of the available audible Quips are still locked for each character.

There are three pieces of data that can be displayed at once, based on which Trackers you unlock and select. Shown here, the Tracker 1 slot was selected on the left side of the screen, and the now unlocked AR Skills Tracker item (shown in the center of the screen) was selected. It'll now be displayed as part of that Legend's stats during the game. A sample of this is shown on the right side of the screen.

Every Legend has optional Finishing moves (known as "Finishers") that are animated movements they showcase upon making a kill during a match. Again, these don't impact a Legend's combat abilities. When a kill is made and a Finisher is used, all gamers who have Legends in the area will see it. Upon selecting a Finisher, you're able to view a preview of it before purchasing it within the Store. Every Legend has one Finisher that comes unlocked and ready to use.

After making a kill during a match, you must manually press the Finisher button/key to activate it. When using a PC keyboard, press the "E" key. On a PS4, press the Square controller button, and on an Xbox One, press the "X" controller button.

Unless a specific Legend's Finishing move is a featured item within the Store, these must be unlocked, one at time, either by opening Apex Packs or using Crafting Metals. Once Battle Passes are introduced into the game, you'll be able to unlock cosmetic items for the Legends by accomplishing specific tasks during matches. Each Battle Pass will exist for about three months, although all items you acquire from a Battle Pass will be yours to keep forever.

Remember, using any of the cosmetic items when playing *Apex Legends* is totally optional. If you're a newb, focus on memorizing the controls, building your muscle memory for the controls, and gaining experiencing by actually participating in matches. Using cosmetic items and Finishers, for example, is a secondary and much less essential skill when it comes to becoming a top-ranked *Apex Legends* gamer.

LEARN THE BASICS FROM TRAINING MODE

EVEN IF YOU HAVE A TON OF EXPERIENCE PLAYING OTHER battle royale games like *Fortnite: Battle Royale* or *PUBG*, or you've played challenging combat games, like *Overwatch*, there's still a significant learning curve when it comes to playing *Apex Legends*.

HOW TO ACCESS TRAINING MODE

To help you get used to the controls and delve right into the action, EA has incorporated a short tutorial into the game, called **Training Mode**.

From the Lobby screen, select the Training option, and then select Training. Next, click or select the Ready button to experience Training Mode first hand. The first time you visit, plan on spending about 15 minutes here. Later, you can return here as often as you'd like, although once you understand the basics of the game, you're better off gaining experience by actually participating in matches.

DISCOVER SOME CORE GAMING SKILLS

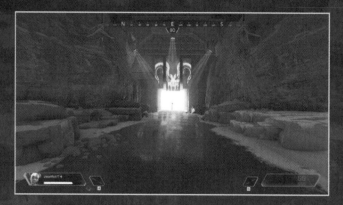

Upon entertaining Training Mode, you'll find yourself in a long hallway. A shadowy figure can be seen ahead. He introduces himself as Bloodhound.

On the right side of the screen (referred to by Bloodhound as the HUD or Heads-Up Display), is a checklist of movement commands. One at a time, complete each item on the checklist, starting with walking forward. Next, sprint (run), and then jump. As you complete each task, a checkmark appears on the checklist.

After completing the initial tasks, follow Bloodhound into Kings Canyon and listen carefully to what he has to say. You'll be given another set of tasks to accomplish, starting with opening a Supply Bin.

As you can see, a new checklist appears on the HUD. It's time to practice throwing grenades and using Health-replenishments items. Listen to what Bloodhound says and follow the on-screen prompts.

Walk up to Bloodhound and the closest Supply Bin that he's standing next to.

After tossing a grenade, you'll be prompted to use a Health-replenishment item to boost your Legend's Health meter.

When prompted, open the Supply Bin and grab the three items within it.

Once you begin participating in matches and collecting multiple grenades and Health/Shield replenishment items, there are several ways to access and use them. One is to access this Ordnance menu and then select which item you want to use. Another option is to use the key/button associated with that item. Your third option is to access your Legend's Inventory screen, select the item, and then opt to use it.

Proceed to the second Supply Bin and open it. This time grab a weapon and the ammo that's inside.

Since you're already in a shooting range area, take a few practice shots using the weapon. Notice that you can shoot without pressing the Aim button.

The next part of your tutorial includes learning how to Ping specific locations, enemy locations, weapons, and ammo.

Alternatively, press the Aim button and you'll have more precise aiming (plus be able to take advantage of the weapon's scope, if applicable).

You'll also need to practice accessing the Ping menu. Using the Ping feature is one of the best ways to communicate with your squad mates during a match. It's even more efficient than speaking with them via a gaming headset (or the microphone and speaker that's built into your computer).

Again, follow the directions from your mentor. Seek out and pick up a second weapon, switch between weapons, and then swap one weapon for another. These are all core skills you'll need in order to survive during a match. Complete the checklist displayed on the HUD.

In this case, approach the dummy and hold down the Revive button. It takes several seconds to successfully Revive a squad mate.

Your next objective is to locate and speak with Pathfinder, another of the Legends. He'll instruct you on how to Revive a squad mate and use your Legend's tactical ability. To find Pathfinder, follow the yellow beacon that's displayed on the screen. You'll need to jump and climb upward across the terrain to find him.

Next, you'll learn how to use your Legend's tactical ability. Each Legend has a unique tactical ability that'll prove to be extremely useful during a match. In this case, you're controlling Lifeline. Her tactical ability involves being able to summon and use a D.O.C. Heal Drone to restore Health to her squad mates.

Continue following Pathfinder's instructions and completing the tasks he assigns. One task is to find and Revive a dummy. During actual matches, you'll often need to Revive your squad mates that get knocked out.

Anytime one of your squad mates gets killed during a match, you have the ability to help them Respawn and re-enter into the match. To do this, approach their corpse and collect their personal Banner from their crate.

Once you have the dead squad mate's Banner in hand, proceed to a Respawn Beacon. You'll see them listed on the Map screen. Shown here is what they look like. It takes several seconds to Respawn a killed squad

Lifeline has the ability to call in Care Packages during a match using her Ultimate ability. Once this ability is fully charged, select it and then choose where you want the Care Package to arrive.

A landing location for the Care Package will be marked. Now find cover and wait for the Care Package to land.

Approach the Care Package. During a real match, when enemies could be nearby, use caution when making your approach. Open the Care Package and grab the item that's inside. In this case, what's inside is a useful Skullpiercer Rifling weapon attachment. The item will automatically be attached to a compatible weapon if you have one in your Legend's inventory, or it will be placed as an unused item in their inventory if your Legend is not holding a compatible weapon.

Anytime you see an item that you don't currently need, Ping it. This alerts your squad mates of the item you've found and shows them its location. They can now choose whether or not to find and grab it for them-selves. Another option is to grab it, find your squad mate, and then share it with them by dropping the item in front of them.

When your training is completed, you'll automatically be returned to the Lobby screen. You're now ready to participate in your first match. Before doing so, however, you're much better off reading the rest of this strategy guide, so you become familiar with the rest of *Apex Legends* before you're dropped into a match and forced to learn on the go.

At any time, from the Lobby, you can return to Training Mode and spend as much time as you'd like there. For example, you can practice shooting with different weapons at the shooting range. When you return to this area, ignore Bloodhound and Pathfinder. Do not complete any of the assigned tasks.

WHAT TO EXPECT WITHIN KINGS CANYON

At the start of each match, all of the squads are placed aboard the Jump Ship and transported to an island. In the future, additional islands or areas may be introduced into *Apex Legends*, but initially, all matches take place within Kings Canyon.

Upon boarding the aircraft, access the Map to see the random route the aircraft will follow across the island. This is depicted using a golden line comprised of arrows. Use this information to help you and your squad mates choose a landing location. Also displayed on the Map are icons showing the location of Respawn Beacons, the Supply Ship, the Hot Zone, and upcoming Supply Drops.

YOUR LANDING LOCATION DETERMINES YOUR INITIAL FIGHTING STRATEGY

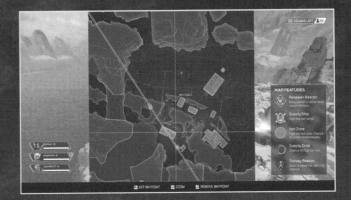

You're able to zoom in and reposition the map to see more detail related to specific locations. Choosing a popular location to land at the start of each map virtually guarantees you'll encounter enemies right away and be forced into combat. In this case, you'll want to reach land as quickly as possible, be the first soldier at your desired landing location, and quickly grab weapons and ammo before your adversaries.

An alternate strategy is to choose a less popular landing location that's away from the route the aircraft follows across the island. This gives you and your squad mates more time to explore and build up an arsenal before being forced into firefights.

The potential drawback to choosing a remote landing location is that you'll sometimes need to travel a great distance to stay in the safe area once the safe circle forms and then begins to move and shrink. Getting caught too far outside the safe circle could become a death sentence if you're not able to return to the safe area before your Legend's Health meter is fully depleted.

Each time a match begins, one of the three squad members is randomly awarded the role of Jumpmaster. This is the person who decides where the squad will land, and when to leap from the aircraft to begin the freefall toward land. The other two squad members can simply follow the Jumpmaster or opt to choose their own jump time and landing location. Especially if you're a newb, it's best to stick with your squad mates. Which squad mate is the Jumpmaster is displaying during the countdown near the bottom-center of the screen.

If your Legend is given the role of Jumpmaster, you can either choose the landing location for your squad, or relinquish this job to someone else, but you'll need to make your choice quickly. Watch for the "You Are Jumpmaster" message to be displayed near the bottom-center of the screen.

As the designated Jumpmaster, it is your job to Ping the desired landing location, choose when your squad should leap from the plane, and then guide your squad to the selected location on the island.

As the Jumpmaster, using the directional controls, control

By keeping their bodies horizontal with the land and their heads slightly upwards, this gives your squad the ability to glide through the air, fall slower, and cover more territory before actually landing. As you can see, the falling speed of the Legends is displayed on the screen during freefall.

As the Legends approach land, their fall is automatically slowed down. They're always able to make a safe landing. What happens next, however, depends on what's happening at the chosen landing spot. If enemy soldiers have beaten you to that location and have already armed themselves, expect to be shot at the moment your Legend touches ground. Be ready to take cover and quickly find a weapon.

Before arming themselves with a weapon (or when a weapon is holstered) each Legend has the ability to punch their opponents who are very close. A punch, however, is nowhere near as powerful as any other weapon, so if the enemy is armed and your Legend isn't, throwing punches as opposed to retreating will likely result in your quick demise.

STUDY THE MAP AND GET TO KNOW THE AREA

Kings Canyon is comprised of many locations—some more popular than others. Some locations are chock full of weapons, armor, and items to collect, while others are more barren.

As you begin exploring, you'll discover wide open and mostly flat areas, regions that contains lots of tall hills, rock formations, and mountains, and locations where clusters of buildings can be found. There are also military facilities, small towns, swampy areas, vast wetland regions, and areas filled with caves.

One thing that's unusual about *Apex Legends* compared to other battle royale games is that a soldier does not get injured or die as a result of a fall. Thus, you're free to leap off of cliffs or hills, or jump from the roof of a building to the ground, and it'll have no impact on your Legend's Health.

In order to seek out enemies, explore, and stay in the safe zone, you and your squad mates will be forced to traverse through several regions of the island during each match. The safe zone is within the white circle depicted on the map.

When two circles are displayed, within the outer circle is the current safe zone. The inner circle shows where the next safe zone will be, once the outer circle shrinks and moves. The area on the Map displayed in red is no longer inhabitable.

Anytime you're visiting the island, look for the Hot Zone. This is the random area of the map that's highlighted with a blue circle. It's here you'll always find the best loot, weapons, and ammo. The drawback is that you're guaranteed to encounter a lot of enemies in this area, all of whom what to be the first to grab the best loot. If you wait too long to reach the Hot Zone, it'll likely be picked clean of anything worth collecting.

Another way to quickly improve your arsenal is to locate and visit a Supply Ship. At the beginning of each match, a Supply Ship lands at a random location, which is then labeled on the Map. The Supply Ship always contain a small supply of some really awesome weapons and loot. Just like when visiting the Hot Zone, you need to be the first to loot the ship to grab what's inside. You can always expect to encounter enemies ready and willing to fight

While it's possible to land on the Supply Ship during freefall, once it reaches its final place on the Map, you can approach it from land and then use one of the ziplines to reach the ship itself. By this point, however, the loot will probably be picked pretty clean.

The Supply Ship has a large outdoor deck area, as well as indoor areas and hallways to explore and loot. Of course, you're likely to discover enemies here, so expect a fight.

You'll encounter a network of already-built ziplines and red balloons throughout the island. Pathfinder also has the ability to create new ziplines that he and other squad mates (or any other Legends for that matter) can ride. To ride a zipline, approach it, look up at the cable, and press the Ride button/key. Keep in mind, it's possible to ride ziplines from a tall point to a low point, across a horizontal path, or from a low point to a high point.

While you can walk or run through wide open and flat areas, some areas will require you to climb over walls, jump over obstacles, open doors and enter into structures, ride ziplines, and potentially travel through portals to go safely travel from one area to another.

Almost all buildings and structures have doors you must enter and exit through, as well as doors inside the structure that lead to other rooms or areas. To open a door, have your Legend walk up to it, face it, and then press the Open button/key.

When a door is already open, this typically implies someone may already be inside, so proceed with extreme caution and enter with your weapon drawn and ready to shoot.

One way to get around the island quickly is to ride a zipline to reach one of the floating red balloons that are scattered throughout the island. Upon reaching a balloon, your Legend will be able to glide through the air, back toward land, and cover a lot of territory in the process. Walk up to the vertical zipline at the bottom of the red balloon and choose to Ride it.

It's a common strategy for enemies to enter into a structure and close the door behind them, and then hide and wait for an enemy to enter, at which time, they'll launch a surprise attack. Thus, anytime you're opening a door to enter a structure, stand to the side as the door opens. Quickly make sure the room is clear before entering and looting.

Your Legend will ride to the top of the zipline automatically.

When they reach the top, they'll leap from the high point and be able to glide back toward land.

Also scattered throughout the map are Respawn Beacons. These are structures where you can bring a dead Legend's Banner in order to re-spawn them after they've been killed. The drawback is that it takes valuable time to find and approach a Respawn Beacon, and they tend to be guarded by enemies who don't want you to revive your squad mates.

Typically within structures, but occasionally on the ground and out in the open, you're apt to find armor, weapons, ammo, weapon attachments, and loot items. Simply walk

up to an item and grab it in order to add it to your Legend's inventory. If it's a weapon attachment that's compatible with the weapon you're holding, it'll automatically attach to that weapon and become instantly usable.

A Supply Bin is another object you'll often find during your exploration of Kings Canyon or other islands that get introduced into the game. These are crates that when opened, contain a combination of three random items. This can include weapons, weapon attachments, ammo, armor, health items, or other loot items. To open a Supply Bin, simply walk up to it, use the Open command, and then one at a time, grab what's inside if it's something you want or need.

Within a Supply Bin, if you discover items you don't need or that are duplicates, be sure to Ping the location of the Supply Bin, and Ping specific items within it, particularly Armor, Backpacks, or powerful weapons that your squad mates might want to get their hands on.

KEY LOCATIONS WITHIN KINGS CANYON

Initially, Kings Canyon was divided up into 23 distinct regions or areas. Each is labeled on the map. In between each region is either an open area you'll need to travel across, a series of hills or mountains you'll need to climb over, or a network of rivers or waterways that you'll need to cross.

Here's a rundown of each map location and the level of loot you can expect to find there. Over time, EA will likely tweak the map, introduce new locations, and alter existing locations, so be prepared to explore.

Locations near the center of the map always tend to be popular, because upon landing there, you're virtually guaranteed that it will not be necessary to travel too far to stay within the safe zone as the match progresses.

During a match, locations that are near the beginning or end of the Jump Ship's route are always sure to be popular landing destinations, since gamers often opt to leap from the plane as quickly as they can or wait until the very last minute before leaving the aircraft. Based on this map, Slum Lakes and Artillery are near the beginning of the Jump Ship's route. Water Treatment and Repulsor are near the end of the route. Wetlands is the Hot Zone, and places like Relay, Airbase, and Thunderdome would be considered more remote and out of the way locations.

LOCATION NAME (LISTED ALPHABETICALLY	AMOUNT OF LOOT TO BE DISCOVERED
Airbase	High
Airbunk	Low
Artillery	High
Bridges	Average
Bunker	High
Hydro Dam	Low
Market	Low
Relay	High
Repulsor	High
Runoff	High
Skull Town	Average
Slum Lakes	Average
South Bridges	Average
South Market	Low
South Repulsor	Low
South Skull	Average
Swamps	High
The Pit	High
Thunderdome	High
Two Fort	Average
Water Treatment	High
West Skull	Average
Wetlands	Average

Regardless of what type of terrain you're currently exploring, always try to use your surroundings to your advantage. For example, crouch down and use walls or objects for cover if you're being shot at. This Legend is hiding behind a vehicle while aiming at targets across the nearby bridge.

Choke holds are areas that Legends must pass through that are very narrow, and then leave them vulnerable to attack. Try to lure your enemies into these areas and then trap or ambush them. A long hallway within a structure is an excellent example of a choke hold.

It's almost always beneficial to maintain a height advantage when engaged in firefights, or when you need to see what type of terrain and potential challenges lie ahead. To climb up a wall or small cliff, for example, face it and press the Jump key/button.

This is a long corridor that's outside, but it also represents a choke hold, because enemies can perch themselves higher up and shoot downward into the open area. The Legend(s) in the alley will have no place to take cover.

Here's a good (higher up) vantage point for the Legend who is waiting for enemies to enter into the long alleyway. As you can see, he's perched high up and has his gun aimed on the entranceway. Once enemies enter into the alley, he can allow them to begin passing through so they think it's safe, and then launch an ambush.

It's a common strategy to stay close to the edge of the circle, but you seldom want to cross the line and enter into

BUILDING AND USING YOUR ARSENAL

WHILE YOU DEFINITELY WANT TO UTILIZE YOUR CHOSEN Legend's special abilities, including their tactical, passive, and ultimate ability, what will allow you to win firefights and ultimately achieve victory in matches is finding, grabbing, and using the most powerful and versatile weapons you can get your hands on.

There will also be times when using grenades or throwable weapons will help you cause massive damage to a specific area or enemy. Certain explosive grenades can also help you lure enemies out into the open. Shown here is a single Frag Grenade (an explosive grenade) that's about to be picked up.

There are many ways to gather weapons during a match. For example, you can raid the crate that's left behind when an enemy gets killed. It contains everything that Legend was carrying before their demise. As long as it's safe to do so, take the time to pick and choose the weapons, ammo, and loot items you want.

Here, the Frag Grenade has been selected as the active weapon and it's about to be tossed. Choose a target and let it fly. Keep in mind, there's a short delay between when this type of grenade lands and when it explodes, so plan accordingly.

Choosing which weapon or ability to use and when are key decisions that'll allow you to achieve victory or result in your Legend's death.

TYPES OF WEAPONS

Weapons typically need to be upgraded using weapon attachments to unlock their true potential. You'll also need to amass an ample supply of ammo for the weapon you're using. Equally important, you need to choose the best type of weapon for the task at hand, based on whether you're about to engage in a close-range, mid-range, or long-range firefight.

In addition to the vast collection of weapons available when *Apex Legends* first launched, ever-growing selection of ways to kill your enemies during a match, success comes down to choosing the right weapon for the job at hand.

WHAT TO CONSIDER WHEN CHOOSING A WEAPON

Your weapon selection should be based on several factors, including:

- How far your Legend is from its target. The farther away you are, the more important it is to have a clear line of sight, while being able to take cover in between shots fired or when you need to reload your weapon.
- Which weapon attachments you've been able to add to certain weapons to enhance their capabilities, ammo capacity, and precision.
- Your personal gaming style and skills. Many gamers are able to master the use of a few guns and rely on those to achieve victory. When you have a gun at your disposal that you're particularly proficient using, use it during particularly intense battles to ensure a favorable outcome.
- Which Legend you're controlling, what their unique capabilities are, and what their core function is during a match. For example, if you're controlling a healer or defensive soldier, leading your squad in a firefight isn't the best strategy.

SELECT THE BEST WAY TO FIRE A WEAPON

All weapons offered within *Apex Legends* can be shot without specifically aiming, simply by pressing the Fire button on your keyboard or controller. Shown here is the Alternator (an SMG).

Even without adding weapon attachments, some weapons allow you to aim down the sight of the weapon when you press the Aim button before the trigger. Doing this improves the weapon's aiming accuracy and allows you to focus in more on your specific target.

Certain weapons also allow you to toggle between firing modes. Each time you press the Toggle Fire Mode button or key, a message appears near the center of the screen (in white) that states which firing mode is active. Single Fire Mode has been selected here. One bullet will be shot each time the trigger is pulled.

While this varies by weapon (and in some cases, which weapon attachments you're using), firing modes for a gun can include:

- **Single**—The ability to shoot one round at a time each time you press the trigger.
- **Burst**—The ability to shoot a burst of several bullets each time the trigger is pressed.
- **Auto**—The ability to hold down the trigger and keep firing until the weapon runs out of ammo, needs to be reloaded, or your target is killed.

Keep in mind, anytime you're running and need to get somewhere quickly, your Legend's speed will increase if you holster the active weapon while on the move. Sometimes, you'll need to travel under something that your Legend won't fit through standing up. In this case, simply crouch down and keep moving.

One of the biggest drawbacks to many weapons is their recoil. The more recoil a gun has, the more you'll need to adjust your aim in between shots.

The longer you hold down the trigger to fire continuous shots, the more your bullets will stray from their intended target. You're often better off shooting in bursts. Every few seconds, readjust your aim, and then continue firing in order to compensate for recoil.

Burst shooting mode was used here from a distance. The same point on the wall was the target, but as you can see once the Legend moved closer to the wall, where the bullets actually landed is a bit staggered due to recoil. The Hemlok assault rifle, capable of shooting three rounds at a time per burst, was used here. The weapon's basic magazine holds 18 Heavy rounds.

LEARN THE DIFFERENCE BETWEEN WEAPON TYPES

Memorizing everything there is to know about each of the weapons available within *Apex Legends* is a cumbersome and difficult task. It's more practical to learn what categories of weapons are available to you, develop a basic understanding of the pros and cons for what each weapon category offers, and to learn what each weapon category is best used for. Then simply practice using various weapons in different firefight scenarios.

Remember, each weapon category uses a different type of ammo, so it's essential that you grab and stockpile the appropriate ammo for the weapon(s) you have on hand.

The most popular weapon categories include:

WEAPON CATEGORY	DESCRIPTION
Assault Rifles	These are well-rounded weapons that tend to have a decent size magazine capable of holding at least 18 bullets at a time. This can be increased using weapon attachments, so you'll need to reload the weapon less often. In most situations, using an AR with the Burst shooting mode will serve you well. ARs use Heavy ammo and typically have a large magazine. Be sure to add an extended magazine and scope to enhance the AR's destructive capabilities.
Light Machine Guns (LMGs)	An LMG will use either Heavy ammo or Energy ammo (depending on the weapon model), and can typically inflict more damage than SMGs, but this depends on which model LMG you're using. These are excellent close- to mid-range weapons, but they can be used in most firefights, regardless of your distance from the target.
Pistols	These tend to be the least powerful weapons in *Apex Legends*. They're best suited for close-range combat situations. To get the best results, go for headshots! If the enemy is wearing a Helmet, it might take multiple direct hits to kill your target.

Shotguns	Shotguns tend to have a small magazine. Each shell breaks up into pellets after being fired. Each pellet that hits its target will independently cause damage. However, the farther you are from the target, the more spread out the pellets will be by the time the target is reached. Thus, Shotguns are better close- to mid-range weapons.
Sniper Rifles	These are ideal for long-range fighting, especially when a powerful scope weapon attachment has been added to the gun. Shooting from a height advantage always helps, and a clear line of sight to your target is a must. It's always easier to hit a target from a distance who is standing still, so try to catch your enemy off guard.
Sub Machine Guns (SMGs)	What's great about these guns is that every time you pull the trigger, multiple rounds get fired. The SMGs that support Heavy ammo (as opposed to Light ammo) can inflict more damage. Since multiple bullets are fired in quick succession (or simultaneously), pay attention to the spray of the bullets. This is lessened the closer you are to your target and can be compensated for by using certain weapon attachments.
Throwable Grenades	These are weapons that must be tossed, so they can only reach so far. Use them for close- to mid-range fighting, but make sure you and your squad mates stay out of the blast zone. Grenades are great for luring enemies out into the open, or when they're already held up in a confined space.

What you want to consider when choosing a weapon is its mag size (how much ammo it can hold at a time); how much body, leg, or head damage each round can cause; how many rounds per second the weapon can fire; how much damage per second the weapon can inflict; the weapon's recoil; and which firing modes it offers.

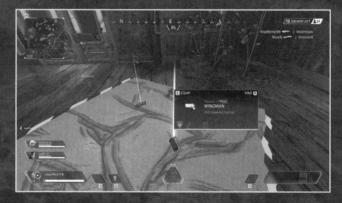

This Wingman Pistol is about to be picked up. It was within a structure, lying out in the open, on the floor. This particular pistol uses Heavy Rounds for ammo, because it's a high-powered revolver. Keep in mind, most other pistols use Light Rounds for ammo.

The Wingman is currently this Legend's active weapon. As you can see from the weapon's display, it holds six rounds of ammo at a time.

This is what the Wingman looks like in the Legend's Inventory screen. Depending on where your squad lands, pistols tend to be the most common type of weapon you'll find early in a match. They're great for close-range firefights, but you'll likely want to upgrade your weapon when possible.

The R-99 is an SMG that uses Light Ammo. It's standard magazine holds 18 rounds, which allows you to put a fair number of holes in your enemy before a reload is required.

The Mozambique Shotgun is about to be grabbed. This may look somewhat like a pistol, but it's categorized as a shotgun.

The G7 Scout is shown above.

As you can see here, the weapon is being aimed in preparation for a shot. This is a quick firing sniper rifle that uses Light ammo. Each standard magazine holds 10 single rounds.

The Flatline Assault Rifle is shown here. Without any weapon attachments, it holds 20 Heavy round bullets per

Here, a scope weapon attachment has been added to the weapon and it's being aimed at a nearby Supply Bin. When an enemy approaches, they can be knocked out or killed from a distance with the help of a powerful scope.

STAY UP-TO-DATE ON WEAPON STATS

Since weapon stats periodically change and new weapons are constantly being introduced, to stay up to date on the stats for each weapon offered in *Apex Legends*, there are several websites worth checking out, including:

- **Gamepedia**—https://apexlegends .gamepedia.com/Weapons
- **GamesRadar**—www.gamesradar .com/best-apex-legends-weapons
- **IGN**—www.ign.com/wikis/apex-legends /Weapons
- **RankedBoost**—https://rankedboost .com/apex-legends/best-weapons- tier-list
- **US Gamer**—www.usgamer.net/articles /20-02-2019-apex-legends-guide /best-weapons-locations

indicate how much damage each direct hit is inflicting, based on whether it's a head, body, or leg shot. When you see damage numbers displayed in yellow, this indicates a successful headshot.

When damage numbers are displayed in red, this means the enemy is wearing no armor, so they should be easier to kill. White numbers correspond to level 1 armor, while blue numbers correspond with level 2 armor, and purple numbers mean the enemy is wearing level 3 armor. Think twice about pursuing an enemy with level 3 armor, since it'll require more direct shots, more time, and more ammo to kill them.

WITHOUT AMMO, A GUN IS USELESS

Each type of gun uses a specific type of ammo. *Apex Legends* offers four different ammo types, including: Light Rounds (displayed with a brown hue).

Heavy rounds are displayed with a blue hue for easy identification.

Energy ammo that can be used with certain types of LMGs and Sniper Rifles.

Shotgun shells are displayed with a red hue. If you know what color ammo you need, based on the weapon(s) you're trying to gather ammo for, the collection process is faster. Don't waste inventory space for ammo types that you don't need. Each time you pick up a box of Shotgun shells, for example, you receive eight additional rounds.

ALWAYS BE ON THE LOOKOUT FOR WEAPON ATTACHMENTS

As you explore the island, you'll discover many types of weapon attachments. Not all of them work with all weapons, however. Thus, you only want to grab weapon attachments that'll work with weapons you already have or anticipate having as the match progresses. Carrying around weapon attachments that you have no plan to use simply fills up your Legend's inventory and wastes that valuable space.

If you come across a weapon attachment you don't need, Ping its location in case any of your squad mates would benefit from grabbing it.

The following chart describes the most popular weapon attachments and explains which weapons they're compatible with, and what each is used for. As you'll see, several types of scopes fall into the "HCOG" category. This stands for Holographic Combat Optical Gunsight Range.

ATTACHMENT TYPE	WHAT IT'S USED FOR	WEAPONS IT WORKS WITH
Barrel Stabilizer	Decreases recoil, allowing for more consistently accurate aim when multiple shots are fired in quick succession.	There are three levels for this attachment–Common, Rare, and Epic. It works with many types of ARs, SMGs, LMGs, Pistols, and Sniper Rifles.
Extended Light Mag	Increases the amount of ammunition that the compatible gun can hold in a single magazine. The higher the capacity, the less frequently you'll need to reload.	There are three levels for this attachment–Common, Rare, and Epic. It works with several types of ARs, SMGs, Pistols, and Sniper Rifles.
Extended Heavy Mag	Works just like the Extended Light Mag but is compatible with a different selection of guns.	There are three levels for this attachment–Common, Rare, and Epic. It works with several types of ARs, SMGs, LMGs, Pistols, and Sniper Rifles.
Shotgun Bolt	There are three levels of this attachment. It increases the fire rate of a gun.	Peacekeeper, EVA-8 Auto, and Mozambique Shotguns
Sniper Stock	Reduces the recoil when used with compatible Sniper Rifles. It also improves the handling of this weapon.	Sniper Rifles including the Longbow DMR, G7 Scout, and Triple Take
Standard Stock	Reduces the recoil when used with compatible guns. This allows for more consistently accurate aim when multiple shots are fired in quick succession.	There are three levels for this attachment–Common, Rare, and Epic. It works with several types of LMGs, SMGs, and ARs.
Skullpiercer Rifling	Increases headshot damage when used with	Longbow DMR and Wingman

Precision Choke	Reduces the spread of ammo shot from compatible guns. To work, the Legend must aim down the weapon's sight when shooting, and it must be charged before use. There are three levels of this attachment.	Peacekeeper and Triple Take
Turbocharger	With this attachment, the fire rate increases on the Devotion weapon, the longer the trigger is held down.	Devotion
Selective Receiver	Change the firing mode of the Prowler Burst PDW back and forth between Burst Action and Full Auto.	Prowler Burst PDW
1x Holo Scope	A rectangular sight that works with all guns. It offers zero zoom, however.	All guns
1x Digital Threat	When attached to a gun, all enemies seen through the sight get automatically highlighted in red making them much easier to spot, even in smoke-filled areas.	Shotguns, SMGs, and Pistols
1x–2x Variable Holo	While aiming down the sight of a compatible weapon, press the Sprint key to switch between a 1x and 2x zoom.	All guns
1x HCOG Classic	A sight attachment that makes aiming easier, but it offers no magnification.	All guns
2x HCOG Bruiser	Provides 2x zoom when looking through the scope of a gun.	All guns
3x HCOG Ranger	Provides 3x zoom when looking through the scope of a compatible gun.	Sniper Rifles, LMGs, ARs, and SMGs
2x–4x Variable AOG	While aiming down the sight of a compatible weapon, press the Sprint key to switch between 2x and 4x zoom.	Sniper Rifles, LMGs, ARs, and SMGs
6x Sniper	Achieve 6x magnification when looking through this scope when it's attached to a compatible Sniper Rifle.	Sniper Rifles
4x–8x Variable Sniper	While aiming down the sight of a Sniper Rifle, press the Sprint key to switch between 4x and 8x zoom.	Sniper Rifles
4x–10x Digital Sniper Threat	Adjust the zoom between 4x and 10x when used with compatible Sniper Rifles.	Sniper Rifles, including the Longbow, Triple Take, and G7 Scout

Shown here is a Shotgun Bolt about to be picked up. This will increase the fire rate of a compatible shotgun.

When used with a compatible weapon, an Extended Light Mag will increase the number of rounds that can be shot before a reload is required. It works exclusively with weapons that use Light ammo.

The Extended Heavy Mag increases the number of rounds that can be shot before a reload is required, but this

A Standard Stock (when used with a compatible weapon) will improve the gun's handling and reduce aim drift. It works with most LMGs, ARs, and SMGs.

The Sniper Stock improves handling and aim, but only works with Sniper Rifles.

This Barrel Stabilizer will slightly reduce the amount of recoil when used with a compatible weapon.

Check out this 2x—4x Variable AOG Scope. It can be used with many types of weapons, including Sniper Rifles, LMGs, ARs, and SMGs.

On the PC, by pressing the Left Shift key, the magnification of the 2x—4x Variable AOG Scope switches from 2x to 4x. Notice the entrance to the building up ahead now looks much closer. Powerful zoom scopes can be very useful for accurately targeting distant enemies, or you can use the scope like binoculars to get a magnified view of what's around.

This is the 2x—4x Variable AOG Scope attached to an R-99 submachine gun. Right now, the weapon is not being aimed, so this is the standard view.

HEALTH-RELATED POWERUPS AND GRENADES

The following are the more popular types of Health and Shield-related powerups and types of throwable grenades you'll discover while exploring the island. These can be grabbed and then held in your Legend's inventory until they're needed. Of course, you should expect additional consumable items to be added to *Apex Legends* in the future.

In most cases, multiples of the same item can be held in the same inventory slot, and then used as needed, one at a time.

The Aim button for the R-99 is being pressed and the 2x—4x Variable AOG Scope is being used at 2x magnification.

HEALTH-RELATED ITEM	WHAT IT DOES	HOW IT'S USED
Arc Star	This is a throwing star that will stick to its target once it lands and then explodes after about 6 seconds.	The energy that's released will inflict some damage on an enemy, plus disorient anyone in the weapon's blast radius.
Frag Grenade	This is a throwable weapon that detonates approximately 6 seconds after impact.	How much damage this weapon inflicts on enemies depends on how close they are to the blast radius.
Knockdown Shield	Provides temporary shielding once a Legend is knocked down.	This item must manually be activated when it's needed. If your Legend gets knocked down, help them crawl to a safe location until help arrives. A Knockdown Shield can protect them against additional attacks for a short time.
Med Kit	Replenish your Legend's Heath meter to 100 percent.	Takes 8 seconds to use, during which time your Legend is vulnerable. No weapons can simultaneously be used, so make sure you find a safe location before using this item.
Phoenix Kit	Replenish your Legend's Health meter and Shield meter to 100 percent simultaneously.	Takes 10 seconds to use, during which time your Legend is vulnerable. No weapons can simultaneously be used, so make sure you find a safe location before using this item.
Shield Battery	Replenishes your Legend's Shield meter to 100 percent.	Takes 5 seconds to use, during which time your Legend is vulnerable. No weapons can simultaneously be used, so make sure you find a safe location before using this item.
Shield Cell	Replenishes 25 HP to your Legend's Shield meter.	Takes 3 seconds to use, during which time your Legend is vulnerable. No weapons can simultaneously be used, so make sure you find a safe location before using this item.
Syringe	Replenishes 25 HP to your Legend's Health meter.	Takes 5 seconds to use, during which time your Legend is vulnerable. No weapons can simultaneously be used, so make sure you find a safe location before using this item.
Thermite Grenade	This is a throwable grenade that releases a line of flames that damage enemies based on how long their exposure is.	There are many ways to use this weapon. For example, use it to seal off a doorway or narrow choke area and prevent enemies from passing through.
Ultimate Accelerant	Quickly restores 20 percent to your Legend's Legendary capability recharge meter.	Takes 7 seconds to use, during which time your Legend is vulnerable. No weapons can simultaneously be used, so make sure you find a safe location before using this item.

An Arc Star is about to be picked up and added to this Legend's arsenal.

As soon as the Arc Star (or any type of throwable weapon) is picked up, it gets stored in that Legend's inventory. Displayed next to the active weapon information near the lower-right corner of the screen, you can now see that this Legend is holding one Arc Star. If he were to collect a few more, the number that appears in the lower-left corner of the Arc Star icon would indicate how many of the item is currently in the Legend's inventory.

Two Syringes are about to be picked up from this Supply Crate and added to this Legend's inventory. Each time one of these items is used, the Legend's Health will be

replenished by 25 points. Syringes are one of the most common types of Health replenishment items available during matches.

While it must be manually activated when needed, a Knockdown Shield will temporarily protect your Legend's front from further attacks after they have been knocked and are incapacitated. Hopefully, one of your squad mates will reach you in time and be able to Revive your Legend before he's killed by an enemy or bleeds out and dies.

After a Legend gets knocked down, if they have a Knockdown Shield in their inventory, it should be manually activated to provide temporary shielding until help can arrive. Only a "legendary" level Knockdown Shield allows your Legend to revive themselves without the help of a squad mate.

When it comes to staying alive when a Legend's Heath and Shield meters get dangerously low, one of the most useful items is a Phoenix Kit. These are difficult to find, so when you can grab one, keep it in your Legend's inventory and only use it when it's absolutely needed. Find a safe location, activate this item, and in 10 seconds your Legend's Health and Shield meters will be replenished to 100 percent.

A Shield Cell can be used to activate and then increase your Legend's Shield meter by 25 points per use. Once activated they take 3 seconds to work. As you can see here, two Shield Cells are about to be picked up and added to the Legend's inventory, however, they can later be used one at a time, as needed. If you check the bottom-left corner of the screen, you can see the Legend's Health meter is currently at 100 percent, and her Shield meter is at 75 percent. Using one Shield Cell right away would boost her Shield meter to 100.

Use a Med Kit to replenish your Legend's Health meter back to 100 percent. This item takes 8 seconds to use, so make sure you position your soldier in a safe place before activating it.

MANAGE YOUR LEGEND'S INVENTORY

At any time during a match, it's easy to switch from the main game screen to your Legend's Inventory screen. From here, you can drop weapons, ammo, or items you don't need or that you want to share with squad mates. It's also possible to see what your Legend is currently holding and learn more about each weapon or item in their possession.

At this particular moment, the Legend is holding a Wingman and Alternator SMG. Ten of their Inventory slots are currently filled, while four slots remain locked. To unlock them, a Backpack upgrade is required. Two of the items currently being held in inventory are not compatible with any weapons the Legend is holding. This is indicated by the red circular icon displayed in the top-left corner of the item icon.

To increase inventory space, it often makes sense to drop items that are not needed, unless they are hard to find and you anticipate needing them later in the match. Next to some item icons within the Inventory slots is a number. This indicates how many of that item the Legend is currently carrying.

Near the bottom-center of the Inventory screen, icons representing the Armor items that the Legend has collected and is using can be seen.

Before switching to the Inventory screen, make sure your Legend is in a safe location, since your focus will be taken away from their surroundings. Try to avoid staying on the Inventory screen for too long, since an enemy can sneak up and kill you.

STRATEGIES FOR WORKING AND COMMUNICATING WITH YOUR SQUAD

IF YOU ALLOW *APEX LEGENDS* TO RANDOMLY TEAM YOU UP WITH SQUAD MEMBERS (STRANGERS), EACH OF YOU WILL HAVE different experience levels and varying skills as gamers, yet you'll need to work together to achieve victory.

When you're viewing your squad lineup at the start of a match, determine who is the most accomplished and experienced gamer. If you're a newb, stick with that person. Pay attention to the number of kills and level of your squad mates.

Becoming a skilled and experienced gamer who is able to achieve kills in a wide range of firefight scenarios using many different types of weapons certainly makes you an asset to your squad. Knowing how to best utilize your Legend's special abilities and skills also allows you to achieve more kills, assist your squad, and ultimately win matches.

If you're new to playing *Apex Legends* and your Legend is designated as the Jumpmaster (the person who decides where the squad will land), quickly transfer this responsibility to a more experienced gamer, or at the very least, accept their landing location suggestions. When you're assigned the Jumpmaster role, the message "You Are Jumpmaster" appears near the bottom-center of the screen.

CLEAR AND CONCISE COMMUNICATION IS KEY

If the Jumpmaster is more experienced and is planning to land in a popular and potentially highly congested area, recommend a less popular landing spot to reduce the chances that you'll need to fight right away. Meanwhile, if you're the most experienced gamer in your squad, and you see the other two gamers have minimal experience playing *Apex Legends*, consider landing in a more remote spot to give them extra time to build up their arsenal.

During freefall, it's possible to break away from your squad, choose your own landing location, and then regroup with your squad mates later. This is useful if you determine that the Jumpmaster has chosen a bad landing location and you believe the squad will likely be killed quickly by landing there. It's also useful if you want to loot a different location and not have to compete with your squad mates to quickly grab the best loot at the landing location.

The key to success when working with your squad is communication! If everyone is using a gaming headset and is able to talk to each other during a match, this makes things so much easier. However, if one or more squad members does not have a gaming headset, you're able to rely on the Ping feature within the game to communicate. Shown here, one of the squad mates Pinged a specific location. In this case, the Ping's yellow beacon appears near the center of the screen, to the right of the truck.

Avoid random chatter with your allies, particularly during firefights. You always want to share important information as quickly as possible. Focus on sharing only the information that's immediately relevant. This often includes details about nearby enemies. Be sure to share the enemy's **distance**, **direction**, and **description** as quickly as possible.

When sharing direction, don't use phrases like "ahead of," "in front of," "behind," "to the left," or "to the right." Unless you know your squad mates are facing the same direction as you, these directional phrases are worthless.

Always share directional information using the compass that's displayed near the top center of the screen. Also, if you're planning on taking a specific action against an enemy, in addition to sharing the enemy's distance direction, and description, quickly summarize and share with your partner or squad mates what you're about to do and how you're going to do it. Even when everyone is able to talk using headsets, it often saves time to rely on the game's Ping feature to quickly share important tidbits of information.

When you're going to push an enemy, for example, either ask your partner or squad mates to accompany you, flank the enemy from different directions, or stay back and provide cover fire, for example. Make sure everyone knows and agrees upon what they should do to successfully execute a well-coordinated and perfectly timed attack.

Be sure to inform your squad mates of actions that might leave you or them vulnerable. For example, announce when you need to reload a weapon, replenish your soldier's health, or if you're knocked down and need to be revived. If you call for help and need to be revived, be on the lookout for nearby enemies, and be sure to warn your allies of their existence and location as they approach.

As a courtesy, when playing *Apex Legends* with a gaming headset, turn off any background noise in the room, such as the TV or any music that's playing. This can be distracting to your squad mates and keep you from hearing in-game audio that's important.

Anytime you're traveling together with your squad mates, don't stay extremely close together. Leave some distance between your Legend and others. This will help prevent multiple squad mates from getting caught in an explosion from an enemy's special abilities or a grenade attack.

After killing one or more enemies, if it's safe, gather near the downed enemy's crate and then pick and choose which items you want to grab. This is a good time to share weapons, ammo, and items with your nearby squad mates, if needed.

Remember that each Legend has their specialties. Make sure you handle the responsibilities of someone in that role. For example, if you're controlling a healer, your squad mates will expect you to Revive them as needed. If you're controlling a tracker, it'll be your job to keep tabs on your enemies and keep your squad mates apprised of their locations.

If one squad member is an excellent marksman using a Sniper Rifle, it should be everyone's responsibility to gather the best weapon(s), weapon attachments, and ammo for that gamer. Prior to the squad launching an attack, the sniper should stay behind a bit, find and position themselves with a clear line of sight to the target area, and use their skills to shoot at enemies from a distance while other squad mates push the enemy's location for a close-range firefight.

PINGING IS OFTEN MORE EFFICIENT THAN TALKING

Instead of focusing on talking nonstop with your squad mates, take advantage of the Ping system, and listen carefully to the in-game contextual dialogue that automatically happens. Each legend, in their own voice, will share important information. As a result of this dialogue and the in-game Ping system, actual conversation between gamers can (and often should) be kept to a minimum.

It sometimes makes sense for squad mates to separate during a match, so that each gamer can build up their own arsenal. From the Map screen, it's easy to set a rendezvous marker, so everyone can easily meet up at a designated location at a specific time. It's also possible to Ping a specific location at a rendezvous point on the main game screen. The diamond-shaped (golden) icon, which in this case was placed near the center of the screen, represents a Pinged location on the map.

It's common courtesy and typically in your best interest as a squad to Revive knocked down squad mates after a battle. If all three squad mates are close together, one can stand guard while the other Revives the third soldier who has been knocked down.

If one of your squad mates is too chatty and downright annoying, you have the ability to mute them. To do this, access your Legend's Inventory screen, select the Squad tab at the top of the screen, choose the player's name you want to mute, and select the Mute option. Unless they mute you too, they'll still hear everything you and the third squad mate says, but you won't hear them. Notice the three icons displayed below the two squad mates. Click on the left (speaker) icon to mute their voice. Click on the middle (Ping) icon to mute their Pings. Click on the right icon to mute their text messages during the match.

Keep tabs on your squad mates. When needed, approach and Revive them if they get knocked out. As you approach a fallen comrade, proceed with caution as the enemy that took them out could still be in the area waiting to ambush you.

After Reviving a knocked squad mate, share a Health replenishment item from your inventory if you have one handy and there's time to safely access your Legend's Inventory screen to drop the extra Med Kit, for example.

To drop an item, stand near the Legend you want to share an item with. From the Inventory screen, select the item you want to drop, and then press the button/key associated with the Drop command. The item will be removed from your inventory and dropped onto the ground, where the Legend standing near you will see it and easily pick it up. If for whatever reason your squad mates fail to see what you've tried to share with them, Ping the item once it's on the ground.

Only risk respawning a killed squad mate if you're able to safely grab their Banner and then make it to a respawn location quickly. If you wind up going too far out of your way, you could get caught up in enemy fire, or find yourself a great distance from the safe zone when the circle moves and shrinks.

WHAT MIGHT BE IN STORE FOR *APEX LEGENDS*

Initially, *Apex Legends* required all gamers to participate in three-player squad matches. In the future, however, it's likely that Solo, Duo, and even many player squad game play modes will be introduced. If this does happen, the same communication skills used when playing with a three-unit squad will still apply when experiencing a Duo or multi-player squad mode.

EXPERT COMBAT AND SURVIVAL STRATEGIES

THE FOLLOWING ARE TIPS AND STRATEGIES THAT'LL HELP you kill more enemies, survive longer during matches, and with practice, earn the title "Champion" at the end of a match.

To invite specific online friends to become part of your squad for an upcoming match, from the Lobby screen, click on one of the two Add Friends (+) buttons that are displayed near the center of the screen.

From your list of online friends that's displayed, choose which friend(s) you want to invite to your squad.

While still aboard the Jump Ship, if you turn around, you can see the enemy squads as they leap off the aircraft and get a good idea of where they're planning to land.

During freefall, a counter that shows how many Legends remain in the Jump Ship is displayed near the top-center of the screen. As Legends leap from the aircraft, this counter decreases. Use this information to determine when and where enemy squads are leaving the Jump Ship. This will help you determine whether or not you're likely to encounter enemies immediately upon landing.

Keep in mind that you can't always see where other squads are landing. As soon as you land, look for a weapon, seek out cover, and listen carefully for enemy activity. You'll often hear enemies before you see them.

If you hear enemy activity before you've armed your Legend, you'll know where you need to avoid—go the opposite direction until you've grabbed a weapon (and ammo) and you're prepared to fight. Also look for signs of activity, such as open doorways or already looted Supply Bins. You'll stay in the match longer if you avoid conflict until you're ready for it.

For help quickly locating the whereabouts of hidden enemies, take advantage of Bloodhound's Tracker, Eye of the Allfather, and/or

Beast of the Hunt abilities. Of course, Blood-hound needs to be part of your squad and the gamer controlling him needs to know how and when to use these special abilities.

Each time you kill an enemy, a crate appears with their corpse that contains everything he or she was carrying. To open the crate, face it and wait for the "Hold [button/key] Access [Gamer's Name] Items" message to appear, then press the appropriate button/key on your controller or keyboard.

Assuming it's safe, open the crate and from the menu that lists its contents, and take what you want or need to enhance your own arsenal. You're also able to Ping the crate, allowing your squad mates to loot it as well.

Remember, there's no fall damage in *Apex Legends*. You can have your Legend jump from any height toward the ground and they will sustain zero damage. This is different from most battle royale games, so it's an ability you may need to get accustomed to using. Check your landing location to make sure there are no enemies below, and then take a leap.

Use the Red Balloons to transport you great distances across the island, or to high-up locations you can't otherwise reach. From a high-up location, use a Sniper Rifle equipped with a powerful scope to knock your enemies. Using Pathfinder's zipline, it's also possible to reach otherwise inaccessible areas on the map.

Some of the more powerful scope weapon attachments have a built-in range finder that displays the distance you are from a target. Use this information to your advantage when shooting, but also when communicating enemy locations with your squad.

When riding along a zipline, to switch traveling directions, jump up, turn around, and then quickly grab the zipline again.

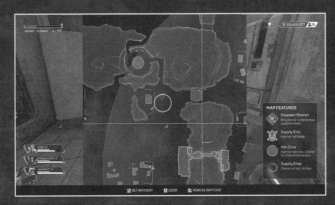

On the Map screen, small blue circles that pulsate are supply drops that are falling from the sky. These typically contain awesome loot. These crates are different from the ones that Lifeline is able to summon. They drop randomly during a match, have red colored markings, and all Legends can see them on their respective maps. The crates that Lifeline summons have blue colored markings. If the crate has brown markings, this means it's already been opened and looted.

An Extended Heavy Mag or Extended Light Mag weapon attachment increases the number of bullets per round that a compatible weapon can carry. These items are color coded. The items with a gold hue can hold the most additional ammo per round. Shown here, an Extended Heavy Mag is being lifted from the crate of a dead enemy.

When climbing up a cliff or ledge, you can grab the top edge and peek over the side to see if the coast is clear before pulling your Legend all of the way up and fully exposing him.

Setting off an explosion within a structure will typically cause doors to automatically open. Just make sure your Legend does not get caught in the blast.

You can also shoot the door handle to open a door from a distance. If you suspect there's an enemy hiding in a structure, stand away from the door, shoot it open, and then toss in a grenade before making your grand entrance with your Legend's weapon drawn.

When in very close range with an enemy, using Melee (launching a punch) will disorient your adversary and send them flying backward. This works as part of a combo attack that includes a gun, but as a stand-alone weapon is not too effective, especially if the enemy is armed and can launch a more powerful counterattack.

Anytime you want to shoot a weapon, you can hip fire (which means shoot without aiming) or aim the weapon and then shoot. Hip firing is less accurate, but it works well in close-range firefights. Wasting time aiming when you're at very close range will actually slow down your response time and give your enemy more time to target and shoot your Legend first. Notice the size of the targeting crosshair (displayed in white). It changes sizes based on what your Legend is doing. If he's standing still and crouching, it'll be much smaller than if he's running with his gun drawn, for example. Here, the Legend is standing still and targeting a rock (so the cross hair is clearly seen near the center of the screen).

Need to make a quick escape from a room or building? It's possible to kick a door open. Multiple kicks will smash the door into pieces. Use the Alternate Interact button/key to kick.

For shooting accuracy, you want the targeting crosshairs to be as small as possible. Crouching down and being skilled at shooting a weapon will help you achieve this. Meanwhile, the faster you're moving, the larger the targeting crosshairs will become.

Shown here, the same weapon is being used, but the Aim button is being pressed so the weapon's targeting scope is being used. It takes longer to aim, but your shots will be more accurate.

Always use your terrain to your advantage during firefights. Jump on items to quickly gain a height advantage and crouch between solid objects to protect your Legend during incoming fire or when reloading their weapon.

A basic Backpack (with no upgrade) can hold eight items. A purple Backpack has 14 item slots, so upgrade when you can. One way to upgrade your Legend's Backpack is to collect one from a dead enemy's crate.

Respawn beacons are displayed on the map as tiny green icons. If a Legend gets killed, one of their allies can collect their Banner and bring it to a Respawn beacon to bring that Legend back to life and re-insert them into the match. As long as there are available Respawn beacons, this is always an option for keeping your squad together once one or more members gets killed in battle.

If you want to increase your XP, expand your in-game experience, practice engaging in firefights, and be aggressive during your matches. However, if you prefer to stay alive longer and increase your chances of making it into the End Game, consider avoiding firefights and enemy confrontations during the early stages of matches.

Which approach you take is a matter of personal preference, based on what your ultimate goals are. Remember, killing enemies gives you more chances to enhance your own arsenal by collecting the loot your victims were carrying.

Before each match, in addition to seeing a screen that shows your own squad's lineup, you'll see a lineup screen for the Champion squad. This is based on the highest ranked and most successful players from their previous match. If you're a newb, these are the enemies you want to avoid. For more advanced players, killing a member of the Champion squad will earn you some bonus XP and help you level up faster. As you can see here, the gamer displayed in the center is the most accomplished, with 3,366 kills.

When you collect a premium weapon from an airdrop, such as a Mastiff Shotgun or a Kraber .50-Cal Sniper Rifle (shown here), they come with ammo. However, you can't restock the ammo once it's used up, so use those weapons sparingly and don't waste ammo. Likewise, many Legendary (gold) weapons that you discover already come pre-equipped with all possible weapon attachments. It's not currently possible to swap out these attachments like you can with other guns.

Keep in mind, the special abilities of different Legends can be used in conjunction with one another when launching attacks. This is referred to as using "team synergy." For example, have Bangalore create a smoke cloud using Smoke Launcher, and then use Bloodhound's Beast of the Hunt ability to see enemies through the smoke.

Anytime you're viewing your Legend's Inventory screen, if there is a weapon attachment or specific type of ammo that you desperately need, point to its empty icon on your Inventory screen and Ping it. This will alert your squad mates about what you want or need. Someone else might already have what you're looking for and be willing to share, or they might discover a location where you can pick up that item.

The Supply Ship that randomly hovers over the island contains a collection of powerful weapons and items. Use ziplines to reach it, if necessary. The location of the Supply Ship is displayed on the map, and you're virtually guaranteed to encounter a bunch of enemies trying to be the first to arrive at the Supply Ship to loot it.

Only approach the Supply Ship if you're ready for a firefight and you think you'll be among the first to arrive at its location. Otherwise the ship will likely be picked clean of anything useful.

Keep in mind, it is possible, during freefall, to actually land on the Supply Ship before the Supply Ship finds its hovering spot over the island. Doing this can give you an

advantage in terms of collecting loot. Also, more than one Supply Ship can arrive during a match. You may discover one at the beginning of a match and another could appear closer to the End Game, for example. Shown here is the inside the Supply Ship (its bridge).

When viewing your Legend's inventory, if certain items display a red icon in the top-left corner, this means that you have no use for that item. If you anticipate needing it in the future, consider keeping it. Otherwise drop it or share it with a squad mate who will benefit from having it.

The Ultimate Accelerant is a one-time use item that increases the refresh time of your Legend's unique ultimate ability. Once you've collected it and it's stored within your Legend's inventory, you must manually activate it when you want to use it. This item is very useful for Lifeline, because it allows her to call in more Care Packages per match. The contents of these Care Packages can benefit all of her squad mates, so if you have an Ultimate Accelerant that you don't need, be sure to share it with Lifeline if she's one of your squad mates.

Each time you pick up an item, a small grid icons appears near the bottom-center of the screen (on most gaming systems). The total number of boxes on the grid correspond to the number of slots in your Legend's inventory (based on your Backpack's capacity). Clear boxes are empty slots. Boxes with a red frame represent slots that are already full. When all of the boxes are filled, you need to drop items if you want or need to make room for others.

When approaching the crate of a dead enemy, you'll notice it has a colored hue around it. This indicates the highest level item in that crate. A level 1 (white) item is Common. A level 2 (blue) item is Rare. A level 3 (purple) item is Epic, and a level 4 (gold) item is Legendary. The higher the level, the better!

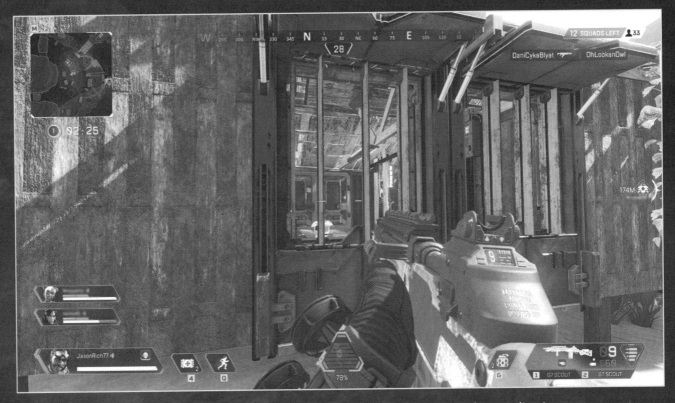

Some structures have windows you can peek through. Before opening a solid door and proceeding into a structure, try looking through a window and see if you spot any enemies lurking inside. You can also approach a closed door and listen carefully for movement inside before opening the door.

The viewfinder or targeting scope of certain weapons sometimes displays the amount of ammo remaining before a reload is required. This is useful if you're raining bullets or shells on an enemy, because it'll show you in advance when you need to find cover and prepare to reload. The same information is displayed in the lower-right corner of the screen.

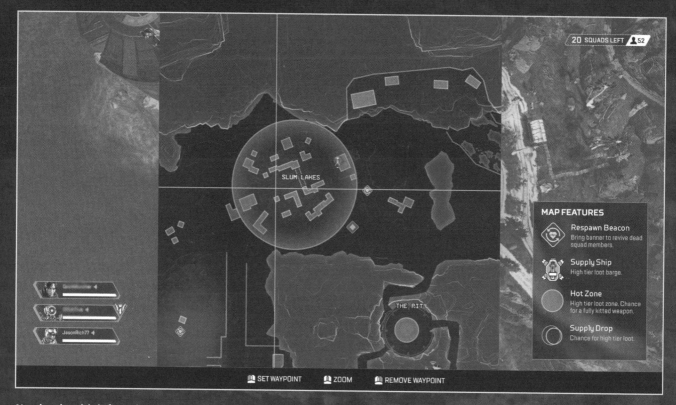

Newbs should definitely avoid the Hot Spots that are displayed on the Map. These areas attract some of the most skilled and ambitious gamers in the match, so you're almost always guaranteed to encounter multiple enemies in this zone.

MORE KILLER STRATEGIES

The following are a collection of additional strategies that'll help your Legend survive longer during a match and kill more enemies in the process.

- As you start playing *Apex Legends*, choose one Legend and get really good controlling that soldier. It's always a good idea, however, to practice using your second favorite Legend as well, in case one of your squad mates chooses your favorite Legend at the start of a match. Don't try to master controlling all of the Legends at once. Doing this becomes a monumental task that gets confusing and requires a tremendous amount of practice.

- If you're a newb, expect that you're going to die often. Instead of exiting a match and returning to the Lobby, stick around and watch the rest of the match in spectator mode. First, there's always a chance you will be respawned by a squad mate. Second, simply by watching other gamers play *Apex Legends*, you're going to learn new strategies.

- Even if you're not yet good at killing enemies, you can still be a huge help to your squad mates by exploring the area you're in and using the Ping feature to alert them to weapons, ammo, and items they may want, and by warning them when you spot enemies lurking about. Only Ping things that are important. If you start Pinging everything, you're going to annoy your squad mates and they'll wind up muting you.

- When making long-distance shots (even when using a powerful scope), you will experience some bullet drop that'll need to be compensated for. If you notice your bullets are landing lower than where you've been aiming, adjust your aim upward a bit to compensate for the distance.

- Some scopes have adjustable zoom levels. In other words, you can switch between 2x and 4x zoom, or 4x and 8x zoom by pressing the appropriate controller or keyboard/mouse key.

- For newbs, the Peacekeeper Shotgun is a versatile and easier-to-use weapon than other types of shotguns. It also holds more ammo per round than similar weapons.

- Anytime you pick up a new gun, any compatible weapon attachments you already have will automatically switch over to the new weapon.

- Using your Legend's Finishing move to end an enemy's life takes a little extra time. This makes you momentarily vulnerable to an attack from another enemy, so before using a fancy Finishing move, make sure the area is clear. Otherwise stick to more traditional weapons for ending an enemy's life.

- Anytime one of your squad mates Pings a specific location to suggest where to head toward or rendezvous, if you then Ping that same location, it automatically confirms that you're on your way to that location.

- When shooting at an enemy, you initial bullet hits will be color coded as you wear down their armor. These colors indicate the level of armor the soldier is wearing. However once you hear the sound of breaking glass, this means the enemy's armor is gone and they're vulnerable. Now is the time to quickly move in and finish them off. Each time you hit an enemy, the number that's displayed corresponds with how much damage your last bullet caused.

- On the main game screen, details related to your Legend's Health and Shield meters are displayed in the lower-left corner. Information about your active weapon and inventory is displayed in a condensed format in the bottom-right corner of the screen.

- In addition to jumping over obstacles it's often possible to climb up objects, structures, and cliffs. Try climbing in order to give your Legend a height advantage for a firefight, or to get a better view of the surrounding area. When facing something you want to climb, hold down the Jump button/ key to begin your ascent.

- Take advantage of a legendary Knockdown Shield to revive your own Legend after they've been knocked down (but before they're actually killed). This is a useful item to collect and hold in your inventory until it's needed, especially if you're a newb or you tend to travel away from your squad mates during a match.

- The Precision Choke weapon attachment allows you to dramatically increase the power and aiming accuracy of a compatible weapon, but it

needs to be recharged in between uses, so plan accordingly.

Some gamers prefer to stay near the outskirts of the safe zone circle. This allows them to look toward the center of the safe zone and see where enemies are positioned by looking in one main direction. An alternate strategy is to stay near the center of the safe zone. This can make your Legend more of a target and easier to spot, but it does often keep you from having to fight and move at the same time when the safe zone circle shrinks and moves.

TAKE ADVANTAGE OF *APEX LEGENDS* BATTLE PASSES

As predicted, in March 2019, the first big update to *Apex Legends* was released. The update included the introduction of gaming seasons. Season 1, called "Wild Frontier," allowed gamers to purchase the game's very first Battle Pass, and unlocked a new Legend, known as Octavio Silva ("Octane").

Octane needed to be unlocked manually, which cost 750 Apex Coins or 12,000 Legend Tokens. To do this, from the Lobby, click on the Legends tab, then click on the Octane tab.

Once he's purchased and unlocked, he'll appear as one of the Legends now available within the game.

At the start of a match, select Octane if you want to control him, assuming one of your other squad members has not selected him first.

MEET OCTANE . . . THE 9TH LEGEND IN APEX LEGENDS

Octane is a man, but he has robotic legs and a never-ending craving to travel fast. In other words, he's an adrenaline junkie. Like the eight original Legends, he has a Tactical, Passive, and Ultimate ability, plus he can use any of the weapons and tools he discovers on the island during a match.

Like all of the other Legends, you can customize Octane's appearance by unlocking and selecting a Skin, Banner, Quips, and/or Finishers before a match. There are many different skins that can be unlocked. The skins, of course, make Octane look awesome, but don't impact his speed or fighting abilities. They're for cosmetic purposes only.

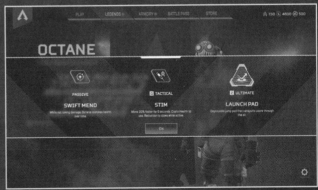

Meet Octane, the ninth Legend currently available in *Apex Legends*. With each new gaming season in the future, expect new Legends to be introduced into the game—each with their own special abilities.

Octane's Tactical ability is called **Stim**. It allows him to move 30 percent faster for up to six seconds at a time, but using this ability depletes some of his Health meter. During a match, Octane has an unlimited supply of Stim, but it can't be used continuously. When it's in use, a green hue appears around the edges of the game screen, and Octane can move much quicker. Use this speed to your advantage. You can quickly rush enemies to attack, or retreat from an area faster than many of your enemies can follow.

His Passive ability is called **Swift Mend**. Over time, this ability is used to restore some of Octane's Health meter. In other words, if it gets drained as a result of using Stim, or from an injury, for example, using Swift Mend allows this Legend to heal himself over time.

The Launch Pad can then be used by Octane (or any other Legend) to quickly catapult themselves high into the air. Simply have your Legend step on the platform. Your Legend will travel straight upwards. While airborne, use the navigational controls to glide your Legend through the air. After this Ultimate ability gets used, it'll take a while to regenerate.

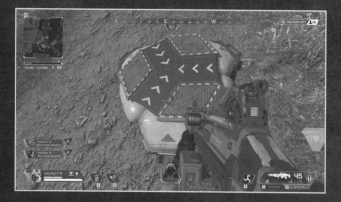

Octane's Ultimate ability is called Launch Pad. When used, a Jump Pad is created and can be placed in any nearby location that you choose.

Not only can going airborne allow Legends to relocate faster, they're also able to use their weapons, so you can quickly achieve a height advantage by leaping up onto a hill or mountain. You can also try to shoot at enemies while flying through the air, but this is a more challenging skill to master.

BATTLE PASSES OFFER NEW WAYS TO ENJOY *APEX LEGENDS*

Moving forward, every three months or so, a new *Apex Legends* gaming season will kick off, and the previous one will come to an end.

During each gaming season, you're able to purchase a new Battle Pass. From the Lobby, click on the Battle Pass. You'll find it along the top of the screen.

From the Battle Pass screen, click on the Buy Premium Battle Pass banner that's displayed on the left side of the screen. To learn what the current Battle Pass includes, first click on the About Battle Pass button.

Each Battle Pass includes 100 levels. As you level up as a player by gaining XP, your Battle Pass will level up as well. Each time this happens (while participating in regular matches), you receive a prize that's yours to keep. However, the prizes offered during a season can only be unlocked during that season. Prizes include exclusive Legend skins, Apex Packs, and unique Stat Trackers, for example.

If you manage to reach Level 97 before Season 1 ends, you'll earn enough Apex Coins (approximately 1,000 of them), which

you can apply to the purchase of the Season 2 Battle Pass. In other words, you can ultimately earn more Apex Coins during a Season 1 than you spent to buy the first Battle Pass, and at the same time, unlock some other pretty awesome loot that will never be re-released into the game.

To reach Battle Pass levels 97, 98, 99 and 100 during Season 1, however, you'll need to play *Apex Legends* for at least 135 hours during the three-month-long (90-day) gaming season, so pace yourself accordingly.

During future gaming seasons, a Battle Pass might include specific challenges you'll need to complete in order to unlock Battle Pass levels, but at least for Season 1, it's all about just playing *Apex Legends* and gaining XP through regular gameplay.

To purchase a Battle Pass, after clicking on the Purchase Premium Battle Pass button, you'll be asked to choose between a Battle Pass or a Battle Pass Bundle. You'll need to first acquire Apex Coins (using real money) to make either purchase.

Purchasing just the current Battle Pass will cost 950 Apex Coins, which is equivalent to about $9.50 (US). If you opt to purchase a Battle Pass Bundle, it'll cost 2,800 Apex Coins (approximately $28.00 US). The first 25 Battle Pass levels unlock immediately, granting you access to all of those prizes.

From the Purchase Battle Pass Level screen, choose how many Levels you want to unlock at once, keeping in mind you'll be charged 150 Apex Coins each. Displayed in the center of the screen are icons that represent the prizes you'll unlock when you purchase the selected Level(s). Shown here, just one Level is about to be unlocked.

Purchasing a Battle Pass is optional, and you can still win certain season-specific items by completing specific objectives. However, to unlock the best prizes, the purchase of a Battle Pass (or Battle Pass Bundle) is required.

Keep in mind, if you purchase just a Battle Pass, you can't change your mind later and upgrade to a Battle Pass Bundle. You can, however, later purchase and unlock one level at a time for an additional fee of 150 Apex Coins (about $1.50 US) each. To do this, return to the Battle Pass screen and click on the Buy Battle Pass Level button.

Shown on this Purchase Battle Pass Level screen, four additional levels are about to be unlocked at once using 600 Apex Coins. By looking at the center of the screen, you'll see icons for the six prizes that'll instantly be unlocked once the purchase is finalized.

Displayed across the Battle Pass screen, near the bottom-center of the screen, is a slider that shows icons representing the prizes that can be won by unlocking each of the 100 levels. Scroll to the right to see all of the levels.

With each new gaming season, expect new Legends to be introduced into the game, and know that as each Battle Pass kicks off, you'll have the opportunity to win and unlock a wide range of goodies. Plus, each new Legend that's added to **Apex Legends** offers something new and creates new opportunities when engaged in battle.

During each regular match, your squad will, of course, consist of three Legends (each controlled by a different gamer). Through experimentation, discover which other Legends Octane should be teamed up with in order to create a more formidable squad. Of course, a lot has to do with the skill level of the gamer controlling each Legend on your squad.

If you opt to control Octane, or any newly added Legends for that matter, quickly learn how and when to use their unique Tactical, Passive, and Ultimate abilities to get the most out of that Legend during combat and exploration situations.

SECTION 10
APEX LEGENDS RESOURCES

On YouTube (www.youtube.com), Twitch.TV (www.twitch.tv), or Facebook Watch (www.facebook.com/watch), in the Search field, enter the search phrase "*Apex Legends*" to discover many game-related channels, live streams, and prerecorded videos that'll help you become a better player.

USEFUL *APEX LEGENDS* RESOURCES

To keep up-to-date on all of the latest *Apex Legends* news and updates, plus discover even more strategies, be sure to check out these online resources:

WEBSITE OR YOUTUBE CHANNEL NAME	DESCRIPTION	URL
Corsair	A gaming accessory company that offers PC- and console-based gamers a nice selection of optional keyboards, mice, headsets, gaming chairs, and controllers.	www.corsair.com
Diegosaurs Twitch.tv *Apex Legends* Live Streams	Diego (known as "Diegosaurs") is one of the top-ranked *Apex Legends* gamers in the world. Check out his live streams on Twitch.tv.	www.twitch.tv/diegosaurs
EA's Official YouTube Channel for *Apex Legends*	The official *Apex Legends* YouTube channel.	www.youtube.com/playapex
Game Informer Magazine's *Apex Legends* Coverage	Discover articles, reviews, and news about *Apex Legends* published by *Game Informer* magazine.	www.gameinformer.com/product/apex-legends
Game Revolution's Online Coverage of *Apex Legends*	Discover news, strategies, and other content related to *Apex Legends*.	www.gamerevolution.com/game/apex-legends
Game Skinny Online Guides	A collection of topic-specific strategy guides regarding *Apex Legends*.	www.gameskinny.com/games/apex-legends
Gamepedia's *Apex Legends* Wiki	An unofficial resource related to all things having to do with *Apex Legends*.	https://apexlegends.gamepedia.com/Apex_Legends_Wiki
GameSpot's *Apex Legends* Coverage	Check out the news, reviews, and game coverage related to *Apex Legends* that's been published by GameSpot.	www.gamespot.com/apex-legends
HyperX	A company that manufacturers a selection of corded and wireless gaming headsets.	www.hyperxgaming.com/us/headsets
IGN Entertainment's *Apex Legends* Coverage	Check out all IGN's past and current coverage of *Apex Legends*.	www.ign.com/games/apex-legends

Jason R. Rich's Website and Social Media Feeds	Share your *Apex Legends* game play strategies with this book's author and learn about his other books.	www.JasonRich.com www.GameTipBooks.com Twitter: @JasonRich7 Instagram: @JasonRich7
Logitech	A company that manufactures a range of keyboards, mice, and headsets. Logitech G is the brand of specialized gaming accessories the company offers.	www.logitechg.com
Microsoft's *Apex Legends* Webpage for Xbox One Version	The official webpage from Microsoft covering *Apex Legends* for the Xbox One game console.	www.microsoft.com/en-us/p/apex-legends/BV9ML45J2Q5V
Official *Apex Legends* Online Support	Get answers to commonly asked questions and seek out *Apex Legends*—related support online.	https://answers.ea.com/t5/Apex-Legends/ct-p/apex-legends-en
Official *Apex Legends* Social Media Accounts	These are the official social media accounts for *Apex Legends.*	Facebook: www.facebook.com/playapex Twitter: www.twitter.com/playapex Instagram: www.instagram.com/playapex
Official *Apex Legends* Website	EA's Official *Apex Legends* website.	www.ea.com/games/apex-legends www.playapex.com
Razer	A company that offers a selection of gaming keyboards, mice, headsets, and specialized controllers (for PCs and console-based gaming systems).	www.razer.com
SCUF Gaming	This company offers a selection of specialty corded and wireless controllers for the Xbox One and PS4 that are used by many pro gamers.	www.scufgaming.com
Sony PlayStation's *Apex Legends* Webpage for the PS4	The official webpage from Sony covering *Apex Legends* for the PS4 game console.	www.playstation.com/en-us/games/apex-legends-ps4
Turtle Beach Corp.	This is one of many companies that make great quality, wired or wireless (Bluetooth) gaming headsets that work with all gaming platforms.	www.turtlebeach.com

YOUR *APEX LEGENDS* ADVENTURE CONTINUES . . .

On February 2, 2019, EA (in conjunction with game developer Respawn Entertainment), made gaming history when **Apex Legends** was released simultaneously for the PC, Xbox One, and PS4. The game immediately attracted more than 25 million players, but that was only the beginning. Since then, **Apex Legends** has not only continued to grow in popularity, but it's continued to evolve as new updates have been released on a steady basis.

With each new update, gamers have been introduced to new Legends, new map locations, and new weapons, along with plenty of other enhancements which continue to keep gamers of all ages entertained and challenged. **Apex Legends** certainly is not the first battle royale combat game to be released, and it won't be the last. However, almost immediately after you start playing, you'll discover that **Apex Legends** offers some unique and cutting-edge features, including the in-game Ping system for communication.

Because you and two squad mates are constantly competing against up to 57 other gamers in real-time (19 other squads), every match you experience is guaranteed to be unique. Hopefully, this unofficial strategy guide helped you get better acquainted with this exciting game and provided information that'll help you achieve victory.

Like any other game of its kind, **Apex Legends** requires practice—a lot of practice—if you want to get really good and consistently win matches. The game does have a steep learning curve, so even after reading this guide, allow yourself time to discover the intricacies of the game firsthand and understand that you're going to get killed often.

As you gain more experience playing **Apex Legends**, you will eventually see yourself staying alive longer during matches, achieving a growing number of kills per match, and ultimately being able to win matches and earn that much coveted title of "Champion." While working toward this goal, don't allow yourself to become frustrated, and don't forget to have fun!

Good luck!